hamlyn cookery club

# Food
# for kids

hamlyn cookery club

# Food
# for kids

First published in 1999 by Hamlyn
an imprint of Octopus Publishing Group Ltd
2–4 Heron Quays
London E14 4JP

Copyright © 1999 Octopus Publishing Group Ltd
All Photography Copyright © 1999 Octopus Publishing Group Ltd

British Library Cataloguing-in-Publication Data
A catalogue record for this book is available from the
British Library.

ISBN 0 600 59907 8

Printed in China

**Publishing Director:** Laura Bamford
**Copy Editor:** Anne Crane
**Creative Director:** Keith Martin
**Design Manager:** Bryan Dunn
**Designer:** Jo Tapper
**Jacket Photography:** Sean Myers
**Picture Researchers:** Christine Junemann and Stevie Moe
**Senior Production Controller:** Katherine Hockley

### Notes

1 Both metric and imperial measurements have been given in
all recipes. Use one set of measurements only and not a
mixture of both.
2 Standard level spoon measurements are used in all recipes.
1 tablespoon = one 15 ml spoon
1 teaspoon = one 5 ml spoon
3 Eggs should be medium unless otherwise stated.
4 Milk should be full fat unless otherwise stated.
5 Fresh herbs should be used unless otherwise stated.
If unavailable use dried herbs as an alternative but halve the
quantities stated.
6 Pepper should be freshly ground black pepper unless
otherwise stated.
7 Ovens should be preheated to the specified temperature
– if using a fan-assisted oven, follow the manufacturer's
instructions for adjusting the time and temperature.
8 Measurements for canned food have been given as a
standard metric equivalent.

# Contents

# Introduction

Cooking for children can be quite a challenge. Their meals need to be nutritionally balanced and attractively presented to encourage them to eat well and in some cases to cope with irrational prejudices and dislikes. The best thing is to start off as you wish to continue. It's important to tempt children to eat as wide a range of foods as possible and to ensure that they get the right balance of nutrients. So, begin when they are very young, when they are being introduced to new textures and flavours for the first time.

When children are very small, eating is just one of the many new and exciting things to do, all with an equal claim on their enthusiasm and time. Some children relish the experience, others need a bit of help. For very young children, give the extra twist of novelty. Cakes and bakes, patties and fishcakes made with animal cutters, or stars and moons, have more appeal than conventional ones. Funny faces always go down well, and sometimes changing the name of a dish will make it more palatable. A Treasure Chest may be more appealing than a Cornish pasty.

As they grow older, try and discourage children from becoming fussy and faddy – so often their dislikes are triggered off at an early age by the look of a particular dish, so presentation is important. But don't force them to eat foods they simply don't enjoy and, if vegetables are a problem, serve very small quantities, one piece of broccoli or carrot and a few peas are much more likely to be eaten up and then eaten another time than a substantial portion. Alternatively, serve vegetables in a blended soup or add them to a pasta dish. Encourage children to help when you are cooking as they enjoy what they have made. They can help by laying the table, washing vegetables and weighing ingredients.

Try to sit down with your children when they eat, especially when they are younger. Don't rush children when they are eating, this way mealtimes can remain fun. Give small portions – too much food piled on to a plate can be off putting and they can always ask for more if they are hungry. Alternatively food can be placed in dishes on the table, so that children can help themselves. Make sure the meal has plenty of variety both in colour and texture and give small piles of individual food rather than mixing it all together.

## Packed Lunches

These can be a problem as so many children seem to have an insatiable appetite for junk food, which so often means foods with too much fat and a high salt content. However, small is beautiful. Little pots of yogurt, individual packs of fruit juice and tiny packets of nuts and raisins have child appeal. Fresh fruit is a must and as an alternative dried fruit is always preferable to sweets. But keep things in proportion and remember that the occasional packet of crisps can be a welcome treat.

## A Well-balanced Diet

A properly balanced diet will give children a wide selection of foods with the right amount of calories to provide energy, as well as all the necessary nutrients for growth and health.

## Food Pyramid

Nutritionists have devised a food pyramid, with essential basic foods like cereals and grains at the bottom, narrowing to sugars and fats at the top. They recommend that we should all eat substantial quantities of starchy carbohydrate foods such as breads, pasta and rice, which provide energy as well as essential minerals and vitamins. The next layer of the pyramid consists of fruit and vegetables and they also recommend eating generous quantities of these, especially in their fresh form, for their mineral and vitamin content, notably vitamins A and C. Meat and other protein foods, and dairy foods make up the next layer and they suggest smaller quantities of foods from these groups, and strictly limit quantities for the last two groups, the fats and sugars. Although children must have some fat in their diets, it is advisable to restrict their intake of saturated fats, found in animal sources. Buy lean meat and use healthy methods of cooking such as poaching, baking, steaming, braising and grilling rather than frying. Limit sugary foods and drinks to special treats and encourage your children to eat fresh fruit and drink juices instead.

# Main Meals

## Sausage Batter Pudding

50 g (2 oz) wholemeal flour

175 g (6 oz) plain flour

1 egg, beaten

1 egg white

450 ml (¾ pint) milk

1 tablespoon Worcestershire
  sauce

1 tablespoon olive oil

500 g (1 lb) cocktail sausages

Mix the wholemeal and plain flours in a bowl, make a well in the centre and whisk in the egg and egg white. Gradually whisk in the milk until the batter is smooth then stir in the Worcestershire sauce.

Pour the olive oil in a roasting tin and heat in a preheated oven, 220°C (425°F), Gas Mark 7, for about 2 minutes. Add the sausages to the roasting tin and stir to coat them in a little of the oil. Pour the batter over the sausages and arrange the sausages evenly in the roasting tin. Bake the pudding in the oven for 35 minutes, until well risen and golden. Serve the batter pudding hot and garnished with watercress sprigs, if liked.

**Serves 4**

*below: sausage batter pudding*

# Pasta Bolognese

3 tablespoons olive oil
25 g (1 oz) butter
½ small onion, finely chopped
½ small carrot, finely chopped
1 small celery stalk, diced
25 g (1 oz) mushrooms, diced
1 garlic clove, finely chopped
50 g (2 oz) ham or lean bacon, diced
375 g (12 oz) lean minced beef
2 tablespoons finely chopped parsley
2 teaspoons plain flour
4 tablespoons tomato purée
400 ml (14 fl oz) stock
150 ml (¼ pint) double cream
500 g (1 lb) fettuccine or spaghetti
salt and pepper
chopped parsley, to garnish
freshly grated Parmesan cheese,
    to serve

Heat the oil and butter in a saucepan, add the onion, carrot, celery, mushrooms and garlic and fry gently until lightly browned. Add the ham and beef and fry until the beef is browned. Add the parsley, and season to taste with salt and pepper.

When the wine has reduced, stir in the flour. Simmer very gently for 10–15 minutes, stirring constantly.

Add the tomato purée and a little of the stock. Simmer gently, covered, for 1½ hours, gradually stirring in the remaining stock.

Stir in the cream and simmer, uncovered, until reduced.

Meanwhile, cook the pasta in salted boiling water according to packet instructions, until tender. Drain the pasta and toss with half the sauce. Transfer to a warmed serving dish and spoon the remaining sauce over the top. Garnish with parsley, and serve immediately with Parmesan cheese.

**Serves 4**

# Penne with Tuna

50 ml (2 fl oz) olive oil
1 garlic clove, crushed
250 g (8 oz) mushrooms, finely sliced
1 small red pepper, cored, deseeded
    and thinly sliced
200 g (7 oz) can tuna steak in oil
500 g (1 lb) penne (quills) pasta
salt and pepper
finely chopped parsley, to garnish

Heat the oil in a saucepan. Gently fry the garlic, mushrooms and pepper for 5 minutes, until the vegetables are tender. Place the tuna and its oil into a bowl, flake the fish, then add it to the pan. Stir gently until the sauce is blended. Season with salt and pepper.

Meanwhile, cook the pasta in salted boiling water according to packet instructions, until tender. Drain and toss the pasta with half the sauce. Transfer to a warmed serving dish and spoon over the remaining sauce. Garnish with chopped parsley.

**Serves 4–6**

# Spaghetti alla Carbonara

3 tablespoons olive oil
1 garlic clove, lightly crushed
250 g (8 oz) rashers of rindless
    streaky bacon, chopped
3 tablespoons dry white wine
3 eggs
75 g (3 oz) freshly grated Parmesan
    cheese
3 tablespoons finely chopped parsley
375 g (12 oz) spaghetti
salt and pepper

Heat the oil in a frying pan, and gently fry the garlic until golden. Remove from the pan with a slotted spoon. Add the bacon and fry for 2 minutes over a fairly high heat until crisp. Add the wine, and simmer until it has evaporated.

In a bowl, beat together the eggs, Parmesan, parsley, and salt and pepper to taste.

Meanwhile, cook the spaghetti in salted boiling water, according to packet instructions, until tender. Drain thoroughly and return the spaghetti to the pan.

Immediately stir in the beaten egg mixture and the bacon, and continue stirring until the heat from the spaghetti cooks the eggs. Transfer to a warmed serving dish and serve immediately.

**Serves 4**

# Macaroni with Ham, Tomato and Cheese Sauce

40 g (1½ oz) butter
1 tablespoon olive oil
3 garlic cloves, finely chopped
175 g (6 oz) cooked ham, finely diced
400 g (13 oz) can chopped tomatoes
500 g (1 lb) macaroni
2 tablespoons chopped fresh basil
125 g (4 oz) freshly grated pecorino
  or Parmesan cheese
salt and pepper

Heat the butter and oil over a moderate heat. Add the garlic and ham, and fry gently for 4–5 minutes. Add the tomatoes and salt and pepper to taste. Simmer for 10–15 minutes, or until well blended, stirring frequently.

Meanwhile, cook the macaroni in salted boiling water according to packet instructions, until tender. Drain and toss with half the sauce. Transfer to a warmed serving dish and spoon the remaining sauce over the top.

Mix the basil with the cheese and sprinkle over the macaroni. Serve immediately.

**Serves 4**

# Macaroni with Sausage and Tomato Sauce

1 tablespoon olive oil
1 large onion, chopped
2 garlic cloves, crushed
500 g (1 lb) Italian sausage, peeled
  and roughly chopped
1 red pepper, cored, deseeded and
  cut into 1 cm (½ inch) squares
750 g (1½ lb) tomatoes, skinned and
  chopped
2 teaspoons dried oregano
2 tablespoons tomato purée
250 g (8 oz) macaroni or rigatoni
25 g (1 oz) butter
salt and pepper

Heat the oil in a frying pan, and gently fry the onion until soft. Add the garlic, and fry until it is beginning to colour. Add the sausage to the pan and fry until evenly brown.

Add the red pepper, tomatoes, oregano and tomato purée, and salt and pepper. Cook gently, uncovered, for 12–15 minutes.

Meanwhile, cook the pasta in salted boiling water according to packet instructions, until tender. Drain well and stir in the butter.

Toss the pasta with the sauce then transfer to a warmed serving dish. Serve immediately.

**Serves 2–3**

# Tagliatelle with Ham, Pea and Mushroom Sauce

50 g (2 oz) butter
250 g (8 oz) mushrooms, thinly sliced
125 g (4 oz) frozen peas
300 ml (½ pint) single cream
125 g (4 oz) lean cooked ham, cut
  into matchstick strips
125 g (4 oz) freshly grated Parmesan
  cheese
500 g (1 lb) tagliatelle
salt and pepper

Melt half the butter, and gently fry the mushrooms until just tender. Season to taste with salt and pepper. Cook the peas in salted boiling water then drain.

Put the remaining butter and the cream into a saucepan, and heat gently without allowing the mixture to boil. Add the mushrooms with their juice, the peas and the ham. Add one-third of the Parmesan cheese.

Meanwhile, cook the pasta in salted boiling water according to packet instructions, until tender. Drain and toss the pasta with half the sauce. Transfer to a warmed serving dish and spoon the remaining sauce over the top. Serve immediately with the remaining Parmesan cheese.

**Serves 4**

# Cheese and Tomato Pizzas

2 x 20 cm (8 inch) thin and crispy
   pizza bases
1 tablespoon olive oil
400 g (13 oz) can chopped tomatoes,
   drained
2 teaspoons dried basil
250 g (8 oz) mozzarella cheese, sliced
4 tablespoons freshly grated
   Parmesan cheese
salt and pepper
basil leaves, to garnish

Put the pizza bases on greased
baking sheets and brush with a little
olive oil. Spoon the tomatoes on
top and spread to within 1 cm
(½ inch) of the edges. Season with
salt and pepper and the dried basil.
Arrange the mozzarella on top and
sprinkle with Parmesan cheese.
Drizzle with a little more oil.

   Bake in a preheated oven, 220°C
(425°F), Gas Mark 7, for 15 minutes.
Garnish the pizzas with torn basil
leaves, and serve immediately.

## Serves 8

*above: cheese and tomato pizzas*

# Quick Focaccia Pizzas with Pepperoni

3 bottled red peppers, drained and diced

3 sun-dried tomatoes in oil, drained and diced

50 g (2 oz) freshly grated Parmesan cheese

3 tablespoons finely chopped fresh coriander

2 garlic cloves, crushed

12 slices of focaccia bread

75 g (3 oz) thinly sliced pepperoni

olive oil, for sprinkling

salt and pepper

Put the peppers and tomatoes into a bowl with half the Parmesan cheese, the coriander, garlic, and salt and pepper and stir together.

Arrange the bread slices on a baking sheet and spread with a little of the red pepper mixture. Top with the pepperoni. Sprinkle with the remaining cheese and a few drops of olive oil.

Bake the pizzas in a preheated oven, 220°C (425°F), Gas Mark 7, for about 5 minutes or until hot and bubbling.

**Serves 6**

# Tuna, Tomato and Anchovy Pizza

275 g (9 oz) pizza base mix

1 teaspoon olive oil

200 g (7 oz) can tuna steak in oil, drained

6 tablespoons tomato sauce

50 g (2 oz) can anchovies, drained

175 g (6 oz) Emmental cheese, grated

12 pitted black olives

Make the pizza base according to packet instructions. Knead on a lightly floured surface and roll to a 30 x 23 cm (12 x 9 inch) rectangle. Transfer the pizza base to a greased Swiss roll tin and brush with the olive oil.

Mash the tuna with a fork and spread it over the pizza base with the tomato sauce. Arrange the anchovy fillets diagonally over the mixture and sprinkle with the cheese. Top with the olives.

Bake in a preheated oven, 240°C (475°F), Gas Mark 9, for 15 minutes, or until the base is crispy and the cheese bubbling.

**Serves 6**

# Lamb Hotpot

2 tablespoons vegetable oil

500 g (1 lb) lean lamb, cubed

500 g (1 lb) carrots, sliced

2 onions, sliced

1 teaspoon grated nutmeg

1 bay leaf

1 tablespoon tomato purée

450 ml (¾ pint) lamb stock

1 tablespoon Worcestershire sauce

125 g (4 oz) red split lentils, rinsed

salt and pepper

Heat the oil in a flameproof casserole and cook the cubed lamb until browned all over. Drain and reserve. Add the carrots and onions to the casserole and cook for about 7 minutes or until beginning to brown. Stir the nutmeg, bay leaf and tomato purée into the casserole with the lamb stock and Worcestershire sauce. Bring the mixture to the boil.

Return the lamb to the casserole with the lentils and cook in a preheated oven, 180°C (350°F), Gas Mark 5, for 1 hour. Discard the bay leaf and season the hotpot with salt and pepper. Serve with Brussels sprouts, if liked.

**Serves 4**

# Shredded Pork Stir-fried

500 g (1 lb) pork tenderloin

½ teaspoon chilli powder

2 tablespoons olive oil

6 spring onions, trimmed and sliced

2.5 cm (1 inch) piece of fresh root ginger, peeled and grated

2 celery sticks, trimmed and sliced

1 green pepper, cored, deseeded and diced

2 carrots, cut into matchsticks

250 g (8 oz) white cabbage, shredded

2 teaspoons sesame seeds, toasted

**Sauce:**

2 tablespoons fresh lemon juice

2 tablespoons light soy sauce

2 tablespoons clear honey

Thinly slice the pork into discs and sprinkle with the chilli powder.

Heat the oil in a wok or large frying pan and cook the spring onions and ginger for 1 minute. Add the pork and cook over a high heat for 2 minutes, stirring constantly. Add the celery, pepper, carrots and cabbage and cook for 4 minutes, stirring occasionally.

Quickly whisk together all the sauce ingredients and pour over the stir-fry mixture. Toss to coat the meat and vegetables in the sauce and serve at once sprinkled with the toasted sesame seeds.

**Serves 6**

# Crispy Cottage Pie

2 tablespoons oil
500 g (1 lb) lean minced beef
1 onion, chopped
300 g (10 oz) frozen mixed
   vegetables, drained
2 teaspoons Worcestershire sauce
1 tablespoon pickle
2 tablespoons tomato purée
15 g (½ oz) plain flour
300 ml (½ pint) beef stock
75 g (3 oz) wholemeal breadcrumbs
1 tablespoon chopped parsley
25 g (1 oz) butter
salt and pepper

Heat the oil in a large frying pan and fry the beef and onion for about 5 minutes or until the beef is browned, stirring occasionally. Pour off any fat from the pan.

Add the vegetables to the minced beef with the Worcestershire sauce, pickle, tomato purée and flour. Cover and cook for 3–5 minutes. Stir in the stock and bring to the boil, stirring. Season to taste with salt and pepper.

Spoon the mince and vegetables into an ovenproof dish. Mix the breadcrumbs with the parsley, sprinkle over the mince and dot with the butter. Bake in a preheated oven, 180°C (350°F), Gas Mark 4, for 30 minutes.

**Serves 6**

# Bangers and Beans in an Overcoat

1 tablespoon oil
4 plump sausages
375 g (12 oz) ready-made puff pastry
1 egg, beaten
425 g (14 oz) can baked beans in
   tomato sauce
2 tablespoons freshly grated Parmesan
   cheese
salt and pepper

Heat the oil in a frying pan, add the sausages and fry gently for 3–4 minutes, turning them from time to time, then remove and drain on kitchen paper.

Roll out the puff pastry quite thinly and cut 4 circles, each about 15 cm (6 inches) in diameter. Brush the edges of the pastry circles with a little of the beaten egg. Put a sausage on each pastry circle and add a generous tablespoon of beans. Sprinkle with salt and pepper. Fold one half of each pastry circle over the sausage and beans and pinch the pastry edges together to seal. Put the pasties on a greased baking sheet and brush with beaten egg to glaze. Sprinkle with Parmesan cheese. Bake in a preheated oven, 200°C (400°F), Gas Mark 6 for about 20 minutes.

**Serves 4**

# Chicken and Courgette Bake

750 g (1½ lb) courgettes, trimmed
   and sliced
75 g (3 oz) Edam cheese, grated
175 g (6 oz) cooked chicken, skinned
   and diced
125 g (4 oz) cooked ham, diced
3 tomatoes, sliced
**Sauce:**
25 g (1 oz) butter
25 g (1 oz) plain flour
300 ml (½ pint) milk
pepper

Cook the courgettes in boiling water for 2 minutes. Drain well and arrange in an ovenproof dish. Sprinkle with 25 g (1 oz) of the grated cheese. Arrange the chicken, ham and tomatoes in layers over the top and sprinkle with a further 25 g (1 oz) cheese.

Melt the butter in a saucepan, add the flour and cook for 1 minute, stirring. Gradually add the milk then bring the sauce to the boil and cook for 2–3 minutes. Season with pepper and pour over the courgette mixture. Sprinkle with the remaining cheese and bake in a preheated oven, 190°C (375°F), Gas Mark 5, for 15 minutes, until golden.

**Serves 4**

# Chicken Bake

2 tablespoons sunflower oil

4 boneless, skinless chicken breasts, cubed

1 onion, finely chopped

1 green pepper, cored, deseeded and diced

3 celery sticks, thinly sliced

300 g (10 oz) can condensed chicken soup

3 tablespoons Greek style yogurt

4 tablespoons chicken stock

1 tablespoon chopped parsley

50 g (2 oz) Cheddar cheese, grated

50 g (2 oz) cheese and onion crisps, lightly crushed

salt and pepper

Heat the oil in a saucepan, add the chicken and cook for about 5 minutes until just beginning to brown. Remove the chicken with a slotted spoon. Add the onion, pepper and celery to the pan and cook for about 5 minutes until the vegetables have softened. Stir in the soup, yogurt and stock then return the chicken and stir well. Add the parsley and season with salt and pepper, then spoon into an ovenproof dish. Sprinkle the cheese and crisps over the top and bake in a preheated oven, 190°C (375°F), Gas Mark 5, for 35 minutes.

**Serves 4**

# Turkey Fricassée

500 g (1 lb) cooked turkey breast, skinned and sliced

25 g (1 oz) butter

125 g (4 oz) mushrooms, wiped, trimmed and sliced

200 g (7 oz) can sweetcorn kernels, drained, or baby corn

**Sauce:**

200 ml (7 fl oz) milk

small piece of onion

small piece of carrot

1 bay leaf

3 black peppercorns

200 ml (7 fl oz) chicken stock

25 g (1 oz) butter

25 g (1 oz) plain flour

2 teaspoons chopped tarragon

1 tablespoon fresh lemon juice

salt and pepper

boiled rice, to serve (optional)

**To garnish:**

1 hard-boiled egg, sliced

chopped tarragon

Arrange the sliced turkey in a casserole. Melt the butter in a small pan over a moderate heat and cook the mushrooms for 2–3 minutes. Spoon them over the turkey with the sweetcorn.

Pour the milk into a saucepan, add the onion, carrot, bay leaf and peppercorns and heat gently for about 5 minutes. Leave to stand for 5 minutes then pour over the chicken stock.

Melt the butter for the sauce in a small pan, add the flour and cook for 1 minute. Gradually add the

milk and stock mixture, stirring occasionally. Bring the sauce to the boil then cook for 2–3 minutes. Whisk in the tarragon and lemon juice, then taste for seasoning. Pour the sauce over the turkey and cook in a preheated oven, 180°C (350°F), Gas Mark 4, for 15–20 minutes.

Serve the fricassée with boiled rice, if liked, and garnish with the slices of hard-boiled egg and chopped tarragon.

**Serves 4**

*left: chicken bake*
*above: turkey fricassée, turkey burgers with barbecue sauce*

# Turkey Burgers with Barbecue Sauce

750 g (1½ lb) minced turkey
1 onion, finely chopped
1 tablespoon chopped parsley
**Sauce:**
25 g (1 oz) butter
1 onion, finely sliced
2 garlic cloves, finely chopped
1 red pepper, cored, deseeded and sliced
125 g (4 oz) mushrooms, sliced
400 g (13 oz) can chopped tomatoes
2 teaspoons dried oregano
1 teaspoon Tabasco sauce
salt and pepper

Mix together the turkey, onion, parsley and salt and pepper. Divide the mixture into 12 pieces and shape into burgers. Cover and chill.

Melt the butter in a saucepan, add the onion and garlic and cook for about 5 minutes until the onion has softened and is beginning to brown. Add the pepper and mushrooms and cook for a further 5 minutes. Stir the tomatoes and oregano into the pan and bring the mixture to the boil. Simmer for 5–10 minutes until thickened. Add the Tabasco sauce and season to taste with salt and pepper.

Meanwhile, cook the burgers under a preheated grill for about 6 minutes on each side. Serve with the sauce.

**Serves 6**

# Smoked Haddock Tart

**Pastry:**

75 g (3 oz) butter

75 g (3 oz) plain flour

75 g (3 oz) wholemeal flour

2–3 tablespoons cold water

**Filling:**

300 ml (½ pint) milk

250 g (8 oz) skinless smoked haddock

15 g (½ oz) butter

1 onion, finely chopped

2 tablespoons chopped parsley

200 g (7 oz) frozen sweetcorn,
  defrosted and drained

2 eggs, beaten

pepper

50 g (2 oz) Edam cheese, grated

Grate the butter into a bowl, stir in the flours and water to make a soft but not sticky dough. Knead lightly then roll out thinly and line a 20 cm (8 inch) flan tin. Prick the pastry case with a fork and chill for 15 minutes.

Line the pastry case with scrunched foil and bake in a preheated oven, 200°C (400°F), Gas Mark 6, for 10 minutes, then remove the foil and return the flan to the oven for a further 5 minutes. Leave the oven on.

Meanwhile, pour the milk into a saucepan and gently cook the haddock for 10 minutes or until the fish flakes. Remove the fish from the milk and flake into pieces.

Melt the butter in a small pan, add the onion and cook until softened. Scatter the onion, haddock, parsley and sweetcorn over the pastry base.

Strain the milk over the eggs and beat together, adding a little pepper to season. Pour the egg mixture over the fish mixture and scatter the grated cheese on top. Bake the tart for about 30 minutes or until just set and puffy. Serve with a salad, if liked.

## Serves 6

# Sailor's Pie

75 g (3 oz) butter

1 onion, sliced

75 g (3 oz) button mushrooms

2 celery sticks, sliced

3 tomatoes, skinned and sliced

375 g (12 oz) cooked cod fillets, flaked

2–3 drops Tabasco sauce

250 g (8 oz) potatoes, thinly sliced

pepper

Melt 50 g (2 oz) of the butter in a small saucepan, add the onion and cook for about 2 minutes. Add the mushrooms and celery and cook, covered, for 7 minutes. Add the tomatoes and cook for a further 2–3 minutes. Place half the mixture in a medium ovenproof dish.

Put the fish in the dish and sprinkle with Tabasco sauce and season with pepper. Spoon the remaining mushroom mixture on top. Arrange the sliced potatoes in overlapping circles on top and cover with a sheet of dampened greaseproof paper.

Bake the pie in a preheated oven, 180°C (350°F), Gas Mark 4, for about 30 minutes. Discard the greaseproof paper and dot the remaining butter on top of the potato. Place the pie under a preheated grill for 4–5 minutes until the top is golden brown.

**Serves 4**

# Chicken Goujons with Tartare Sauce

500 g (1 lb) boneless, skinless chicken
  breasts
25 g (1 oz) plain flour
2 eggs, beaten
125 g (4 oz) fresh white breadcrumbs
oil, for deep-frying
salt and pepper
**Sauce:**
150 ml (¼ pint) mayonnaise
4 baby gherkins, finely chopped
1 tablespoon capers, finely chopped

Cut the chicken into thin strips.
Season the flour with salt and
pepper, add the strips of chicken and
toss together to coat. Dip the chicken
in the egg then coat it in the
breadcrumbs.

Heat the oil in a deep-fryer or
saucepan and cook the goujons in
batches for about 3 minutes each
until golden and cooked through.
Drain the goujons on kitchen paper
and keep them warm.

To make the sauce, stir all the
ingredients together in a small bowl
and serve with the goujons.

**Serves 4**

# Boston Bean Stew

15 g (½ oz) butter
1 onion, chopped
250 g (8 oz) lean ham, trimmed and
  cubed
400 g (13 oz) can chopped tomatoes
425 g (14 oz) can baked beans in
  tomato sauce
125 g (4 oz) mushrooms, wiped and
  sliced
1 tablespoon pickle

Melt the butter in a large saucepan,
add the onion and ham and cook for
about 3 minutes. Add the tomatoes,
baked beans and mushrooms. Stir in
the pickle, then partially cover the
pan and simmer the stew for about
20 minutes, stirring occasionally.

Divide the stew between
individual serving plates and serve
with slices of French bread, if liked.

**Serves 4**

---

*above: boston bean stew*
*right: chicken goujons with tartare
sauce*

# Vegetarian Meals

## Tagliatelle with Chickpea and Tomato Sauce

400 g (13 oz) can chickpeas, rinsed and drained
6 tablespoons olive oil
1 small onion, finely chopped
1 celery stick, diced
2 garlic cloves, finely chopped

750 g (1½ lb) canned chopped tomatoes
2 tablespoons chopped flat leaf parsley
1 teaspoon chopped rosemary
375 g (12 oz) tagliatelle
4 tablespoons freshly grated Parmesan cheese
salt and pepper

Purée half the chickpeas in a food processor or blender, adding a little water if necessary.

Heat the oil in a saucepan and cook the onion and celery for about 5 minutes, until softened but not brown. Add the garlic to the pan and cook for a further 2 minutes. Stir the tomatoes into the pan with the parsley and rosemary and simmer the mixture for 10 minutes until thickened. Add the puréed and whole chickpeas and simmer for 5 minutes. Season the sauce to taste.

Meanwhile, cook the tagliatelle in lightly salted boiling water according to packet instructions. Drain thoroughly. Toss the pasta with half the chickpea sauce and half the cheese.

Transfer the pasta to a warmed serving dish and spoon the remaining sauce over the top. Serve with the remaining cheese.

**Serves 6**

# Pasta with Salsa Primavera

125 g (4 oz) butter

1 onion, chopped

1 carrot, diced

1 celery stalk, diced

125 g (4 oz) peas

2 tomatoes, skinned and chopped

1 large courgette, cut into
   1 cm (½ inch) cubes

125 g (4 oz) fine asparagus stalks,
   chopped

300 ml (½ pint) double cream

500 g (1 lb) fettuccine

50 g (2 oz) freshly grated Parmesan
   cheese

2 tablespoons chopped flat leaf
   parsley

salt and pepper

Melt 50 g (2 oz) of the butter in a saucepan, add the onion, carrot and celery and cook for about 5 minutes, until softened. Add the peas, tomatoes and courgette and cook gently for 5 minutes. Add the asparagus and cook for 1 further minute.

Stir the cream into the saucepan and simmer gently until reduced by half. Season to taste with salt and pepper. Cook the pasta in salted boiling water according to packet instructions. Drain and toss with the remaining butter, the cheese, parsley and half the sauce. Transfer to a warmed serving dish and spoon the remaining sauce on top.

## Serves 6

# Tomato and Vegetable Lasagne

1 small aubergine, sliced
2 tablespoons olive oil
2 onions, sliced
1 small head of celery, trimmed and
  chopped
250 g (8 oz) mushrooms, quartered
750 g (1½ lb) canned chopped
  tomatoes
125 g (4 oz) broad beans, shelled
1 bay leaf
1 teaspoon caster sugar
175 g (6 oz) no pre-cook lasagne
  verdi

300 ml (½ pint) natural yogurt
125 g (4 oz) Edam cheese, grated
2 tablespoons rolled oats
salt and pepper

Sprinkle the aubergine slices with salt, put them in a colander and leave to stand for 30 minutes. Rinse and drain well then pat dry on kitchen paper.

Heat the oil in a saucepan and cook the onion and celery for about 5 minutes, until softened. Add the mushrooms and aubergine and cook for a further 5 minutes. Stir in the tomatoes and beans and bring the mixture to the boil. Add the bay leaf and sugar and simmer for 25 minutes. Discard the bay leaf and season with salt and pepper.

Spoon half the vegetable mixture into an ovenproof dish and cover with a layer of lasagne sheets, then add the remaining vegetable mixture and another layer of lasagne. Mix together the yogurt and cheese and spoon over the lasagne, spread the sauce evenly and sprinkle with the rolled oats.

Cook the lasagne in a preheated oven, 180°C (350°F), Gas Mark 4, for 45 minutes. Serve with a salad, if liked.

**Serves 6**

*below: tomato and vegetable lasagne*

# Gnocchi with Tomato Sauce

1 litre (1¾ pints) milk
200 g (7 oz) semolina
125 g (4 oz) freshly grated Parmesan
  cheese
25 g (1 oz) butter
2 egg yolks
¼ teaspoon grated nutmeg
salt and pepper
1 tablespoon chopped oregano, to
  garnish
**Sauce:**
500 g (1 lb) tomatoes, skinned and
  chopped
1 tablespoon fresh lemon juice
2 tablespoons tomato purée
1 teaspoon soft light brown sugar
150 ml (¼ pint) vegetable stock

Bring the milk to the boil in a saucepan and gradually stir in the semolina. Simmer very gently for 15 minutes, stirring frequently, until the mixture thickens. Remove from the heat and beat in half the cheese, the butter and egg yolks and season with a little salt.

Spread the gnocchi mixture in a dampened baking tray to a depth of 1 cm (½ inch) and smooth the surface. Cover and leave to cool completely.

Using a 6 cm (2½ inch) biscuit cutter, cut out rounds of the gnocchi mixture. Arrange the rounds in a buttered shallow baking dish. Sprinkle with the nutmeg. Bake in a preheated oven, 230°C (450°F), Gas Mark 8, for 20 minutes.

Meanwhile, prepare the sauce. Put all the ingredients into a saucepan and bring to the boil. Simmer for 20 minutes or until the mixture has thickened, stirring occasionally. Season to taste with salt and pepper.

Serve the gnocchi garnished with the oregano with the sauce in a separate bowl.

**Serves 6**

# Wholemeal Vegetable Samosas

**Filling:**
3 carrots, diced
4 potatoes, diced
120 ml (4 fl oz) boiling water
1 teaspoon curry powder
6 fresh spinach leaves, finely chopped
salt and pepper
**Pastry:**
375 g (12 oz) self-raising wholemeal
  flour
75 g (3 oz) butter
about 200 ml (7 fl oz) cold water

Put the carrots and potatoes into a large saucepan, cover with cold water and add the curry powder and a little salt. Bring to the boil and simmer for about 10 minutes, shaking the pan occasionally. Add the spinach leaves and remove the pan from the heat.

Meanwhile, prepare the pastry. Put the flour into a bowl and rub in the butter until the mixture resembles breadcrumbs. Stir in sufficient water to form a soft but not sticky dough.

Knead the dough lightly on a floured surface and divide it into three pieces. Roll one-third to a 23 x 18 cm (9 x 7 inch) rectangle. Spread one-third of the vegetable mixture down the centre of the rectangle. Moisten the edges of the rectangle with a little water and bring the long edges together. Press the edges to seal.

Dust a knife with a little flour and cut the vegetable filled pastry into 3 triangles. Press the cut edges together, to seal the samosas. Repeat this with the remaining pastry and filling.

Arrange the samosas on a baking sheet and bake in a preheated oven, 200°C (400°F), Gas Mark 6, for 20 minutes or until the pastry is crisp and golden.

**Makes 9**

# Vegetable Kebabs

1 aubergine, cut into 2.5 cm (1 inch)
   cubes
2 medium courgettes, cut into 2.5 cm
   (1 inch) cubes
125 g (4 oz) button mushrooms
1 small green pepper, cored,
   deseeded and cut into 2.5 cm
   (1 inch) squares
1 small red pepper, cored, deseeded
   and cut into 2.5 cm (1 inch) squares
12 cherry tomatoes
5 tablespoons barbecue sauce
salt

Place the aubergine and courgette cubes in a colander and sprinkle with salt. Arrange the colander over a plate and leave to stand for 30 minutes. Rinse and pat dry.

Bring a large saucepan of water to the boil and add the aubergine, courgettes, mushrooms and peppers. When the water returns to the boil drain the vegetables.

When the vegetables are cool enough to handle, thread them on to 4 kebab skewers with the cherry tomatoes and arrange in a shallow dish. Spoon the sauce over the vegetables and turn to coat

completely. Leave to stand for at least 10 minutes. Lift the kebabs out of the sauce and cook under a preheated grill for 5 minutes. Brush with a little barbecue sauce and return the kebabs to the grill for a further 5 minutes, or until the vegetables are tender.

Heat the remaining barbecue sauce and serve with the kebabs.

**Serves 4**

# Egg and Beansprout Tacos

6 tacos shells
lettuce leaves, to garnish
**Filling 1:**
7 eggs
3 tablespoons milk
15 g (½ oz) butter
1 tomato, chopped
2 tablespoons chopped parsley
salt and pepper

**Filling 2:**
1 tablespoon olive oil
300 g (10 oz) bean sprouts
1–2 tablespoons soy sauce

Warm the taco shells in a preheated oven, 110°C (225°F), Gas Mark ¼, while preparing the fillings.

To make filling 1, whisk the eggs and milk with salt and pepper. Melt the butter in a saucepan and stir in the egg mixture. Cook gently, stirring, until the eggs have cooked. Stir in the chopped parsley.

To make filling 2, heat the oil and quickly stir-fry the bean sprouts. Add the soy sauce and a little salt and pepper, if necessary.

Divide the bean sprout mixture between the warmed taco shells and top with the scrambled eggs and tomato slices. Serve the tacos garnished with lettuce leaves.

**Serves 6**

# Sweetcorn Fritters

50 g (2 oz) wholemeal flour
1½ teaspoons baking powder
½ teaspoon salt
375 g (12 oz) canned sweetcorn, rinsed and drained
1 teaspoon clear honey
3 eggs, separated
150 ml (¼ pint) natural yogurt
1 tablespoon chopped parsley
pepper
sunflower oil, for frying
2 sliced tomatoes, to garnish

Sift the flour into a mixing bowl with the baking powder and salt, returning any bran to the bowl. Make a well in the centre and add the sweetcorn, honey, egg yolks, yogurt, parsley and pepper. Stir well to mix evenly. Whisk the egg whites until stiff but not dry then fold them into the sweetcorn mixture.

Heat a little oil in a frying pan. Spoon 2–3 tablespoons of the sweetcorn mixture in rounds into the pan and cook for 2 minutes or until golden underneath. Turn them over and cook on the other side until golden. Drain the fritters on kitchen paper and keep warm while frying the remaining mixture.

Serve the fritters garnished with tomato slices.

**Makes about 12**

# Stir-fried Vegetable Rice

300 g (10 oz) brown long-grain rice
1½ tablespoons olive oil
125 g (4 oz) carrots, scrubbed and cut into matchsticks
125 g (4 oz) small button mushrooms, thinly sliced
1 small green pepper, cored, deseeded and thinly sliced
3 spring onions, finely sliced
50 g (2 oz) frozen peas
4 eggs, beaten
2 tablespoons soy sauce
salt and pepper
spring onion curls, to garnish (optional)

Cook the rice in a saucepan of lightly salted boiling water according to packet instructions. Drain and set aside.

Heat 2 teaspoons of the oil in a wok or large frying pan. Add the carrots, mushrooms, pepper, spring onions and peas to the wok and cook for 3 minutes, stirring frequently. Remove from the wok.

Heat a little more of the oil in the wok and pour in the beaten eggs. Cook until lightly browned, breaking up the eggs into smallish pieces. Remove from the wok.

Add the remaining oil to the wok and stir-fry the cooked rice for 2 minutes. Stir in the soy sauce. Return the vegetables and eggs to the wok and stir them together gently over a low heat. Season with salt and pepper and serve piping hot, garnished with spring onion curls if liked.

**Serves 4**

# Potato Skins with Soured Cream Dip

6 large potatoes, with unblemished skins
4 tablespoons olive oil
150 ml (¼ pint) soured cream
1 teaspoon snipped fresh chives
salt and pepper

Cut the potatoes into six pieces. Peel the potato pieces thickly and carefully. Put the potato skins into a bowl and drizzle with oil. (Use the potato flesh in another recipe.) Drain the potato skins. Arrange them on a baking sheet and bake in a preheated oven, 200°C (400°F), Gas Mark 6, for 20–25 minutes, turning them occasionally.

Meanwhile, to make the dip, beat together the cream, chives and salt and pepper.

Serve the hot crisp potato skins with the dip.

**Serves 4**

# Farmhouse Omelette

2 tablespoons olive oil

1 onion, chopped

½ green or red pepper, cored, deseeded and sliced

2 potatoes, cooked and diced

50 g (2 oz) green beans, cooked and sliced

125 g (4 oz) mushrooms, sliced

6 cherry tomatoes, halved

1 tablespoon chopped basil

6 eggs

4 tablespoons water

salt and pepper

1 tomato, sliced, to serve

basil sprigs, to garnish

Heat the oil in a large frying pan and cook the onion and pepper for 5 minutes. Stir in the potatoes, beans, mushrooms, tomatoes and basil. Whisk the eggs and water in a bowl and season with salt and pepper. Pour the eggs over the vegetable mixture and cook over a moderate heat until the eggs are almost set. Put the pan under a preheated grill and cook until the top of the omelette is set. Cut the into 4 and serve with the tomato and garnish with basil sprigs.

### Serves 4

*above: farmhouse omelette*

# Calzone

250 g (8 oz) strong plain wholemeal
   flour
250 g (8 oz) strong plain white
   flour
1 teaspoon salt
1 teaspoon caster sugar
1 sachet easy-blend yeast
1 egg, beaten
3 tablespoons sunflower oil
300 ml (½ pint) warm water
beaten egg, to glaze
1 tablespoon sesame seeds

**Filling:**
1 tablespoon olive oil
3 onions, chopped
400 g (13 oz) can tomatoes
1 tablespoon tomato purée
2 teaspoons caster sugar
1 tablespoon chopped marjoram
175 g (6 oz) flat field mushrooms,
   chopped
175 g (6 oz) green pepper, cored,
   deseeded and chopped
250 g (8 oz) mozzarella cheese, sliced

Put the flours into a bowl with the salt, sugar and yeast. Make a well in the centre and add the egg, oil and milk. Mix to a soft but not sticky dough. Knead for 5 minutes then turn the dough into an oiled bowl and cover with oiled clingfilm. Leave in a warm place for 45 minutes.

Meanwhile, heat the oil for the filling and cook the onions gently for about 10 minutes until golden. Add the tomatoes with their juice, tomato purée, sugar and marjoram. Cook for about 10 minutes, stirring occasionally. Season with salt and pepper then leave to cool.

Turn the dough on to a lightly floured surface and roll to a rectangle measuring 50 x 25 cm (20 x 10 inches). Spread half the tomato mixture over half the dough to within 1 cm (½ inch) of the edge. Cover with the mushrooms, then the peppers. Arrange the mozzarella slices on top then spoon on the remaining tomato mixture. Brush the edge of the dough with a little beaten egg and fold the dough over to form a pillow. Press the dough edges together well to seal. Transfer to a greased baking sheet and glaze the dough with beaten egg and sprinkle with sesame seeds.

Bake the calzone in a preheated oven, 200°C (400°F), Gas Mark 6, for 20 minutes then reduce the oven temperature to 180°C (350°F), Gas Mark 4 and cook for a further 20 minutes. Serve in slices.

**Serves 6**

# Three Cheese Pizza

375 g (12 oz) strong plain flour
1 sachet easy-blend dried yeast
½ teaspoon salt
125 ml (4 fl oz) warm water
90 g (3½ oz) Parmesan cheese
90 g (3½ oz) Gruyère cheese
40 g (1½ oz) Pecorino cheese
2 eggs, beaten
olive oil, for brushing
oregano sprigs, to garnish

Sift 125 g (4 oz) of the flour into a bowl and add the yeast and salt. Stir in 4–5 tablespoons of the water and knead until smooth. Transfer to an oiled bowl and cover with oiled clingfilm. Leave in a warm place for 15 minutes.

Grate 50 g (2 oz) of the Parmesan and half the Gruyère into a bowl. Dice the remaining cheese and add to the grated cheese. Stir in the eggs and the remaining flour. Mix in the remaining water. Add the dough to the cheese mixture and knead for about 10 minutes. Return the

dough to the bowl, cover and leave to rise for about 45 minutes.

Roll out the dough to a 20 cm (8 inch) circle. Place on a greased perforated pizza pan and leave to rise for 40 minutes.

Bake the pizza in a preheated oven, 200°C (400°F) Gas Mark 6, for 20–25 minutes. To serve, brush with oil and sprinkle with oregano.

**Serves 6**

*left: calzone*
*above: three cheese pizza*

# Pizza alla Napoletana

275 g (9 oz) pizza base mix

500 g (1 lb) tomatoes, skinned and roughly chopped

1 garlic clove, finely chopped

250 g (8 oz) mozzarella cheese, sliced

1 tablespoon black olives, pitted and chopped or 6 anchovy fillets, split lengthways

1 tablespoon finely chopped oregano

1 tablespoon olive oil

salt and pepper

Prepare the pizza base according to packet instructions. Roll out the dough to a 30 cm (12 inch) circle and transfer to a greased pizza pan.

Mix together the tomatoes and garlic and season with a little salt and pepper. Spoon over the pizza base. Top with the mozzarella and olives, or anchovy fillets. Sprinkle with the oregano and drizzle with a little oil.

Bake the pizza in a preheated oven, 240°C (475°F), Gas Mark 9, for 15–20 minutes.

**Serves 6**

# Crisp Lentil Patties

1 tablespoon olive oil

1 onion, thinly sliced

1 green pepper, cored, deseeded and finely chopped

1 teaspoon ground cumin

1 teaspoon ground coriander

375 g (12 oz) can green lentils, rinsed and drained

1 egg, beaten

125 g (4 oz) jumbo rolled oats

sunflower oil, for shallow-frying

salt and pepper

Heat the oil in a saucepan, add the onion and cook for about 5 minutes, until softened but not brown. Add the pepper and cook for a further 5 minutes. Stir in the cumin, coriander and lentils and season with salt and pepper. Leave until cool enough to handle.

Shape the lentil mixture into 10 flat cakes. Pour the egg on to a shallow plate and sprinkle the oats on to another. Dip each lentil cake first in the egg then the oats, to coat completely.

Heat the sunflower oil in a frying pan and fry the patties for about 3 minutes on each side. You will have to do this in batches. Drain well on kitchen paper and keep hot while cooking the rest.

**Makes 10**

# Bean and Pasta Curry

1 tablespoon vegetable oil

3 onions, chopped

2 garlic cloves, finely chopped

3 tablespoons mild curry powder

½ teaspoon ground cumin

½ teaspoon ground coriander

½ teaspoon ground chilli

2 teaspoons grated fresh root ginger

2 tablespoons wholemeal flour

900 ml (1½ pints) vegetable stock

1 tablespoon fresh lemon juice

150 g (5 oz) fusilli pasta

2 x 400 g (13 oz) cans red kidney
    beans, rinsed and drained

salt and pepper

Heat the oil in a saucepan, add the onion and garlic and cook for 5 minutes until softened but not brown. Stir in the curry powder, cumin, coriander, chilli, ginger and flour. Cook for 1 minute.

Pour in the stock and lemon juice and bring to the boil. Cover the pan and simmer gently for 25 minutes.

Season if necessary. The sauce can be cooled, then chilled and reheated the next day – the flavours will develop if it is kept.

When you are ready to serve, cook the pasta in lightly salted boiling water according to packet instructions. Reheat the sauce with the kidney beans and stir in the pasta.

## Serves 4

*left: pizza alla napoletana*
***above:*** *bean and pasta curry*

# Gougere with Ratatouille

**Pastry:**

50 g (2 oz) butter

150 ml (¼ pint) water

65 g (2½ oz) plain wholemeal flour

2 eggs, beaten

½ teaspoon English mustard

50 g (2 oz) Cheddar cheese, grated

salt and pepper

1 tablespoon chopped parsley,
  to garnish

**Ratatouille filling:**

1 tablespoon vegetable oil

1 large onion, roughly chopped

1 aubergine, cut into 2.5 cm (1 inch)
  cubes

3 small courgettes, sliced

1 green pepper, cored, deseeded and
  diced

1 red pepper, cored, deseeded and
  diced

300 g (10 oz) tomatoes, skinned,
  quartered and deseeded

2 tablespoons tomato purée

1 teaspoon sugar

1 tablespoon chopped basil

To make the pastry, put the butter and water into a saucepan with a large pinch of salt. Heat the pan gently until the butter has melted then bring to the boil. Meanwhile, sift the flour twice. As soon as the water boils remove the pan from the heat and quickly add the flour. Beat the mixture with a wooden spoon until a ball forms. Leave to stand for about 5 minutes.

Gradually whisk in the beaten egg then the mustard and cheese. Spoon the mixture into a 25 cm (10 inch) round on a lightly greased and floured baking sheet. Bake in a preheated oven, 220°C (425°F), Gas Mark 7, for about 40 minutes until the ring is puffy and brown.

Meanwhile prepare the ratatouille filling. Heat the oil in a saucepan, add the onion and cook for about 5 minutes, until softened but not brown. Add the aubergine, courgettes, peppers and tomatoes. Stir in the tomato purée, sugar and basil and bring the ratatouille to the boil. Lower the heat, cover the pan and simmer for about 15 minutes, stirring the mixture occasionally to prevent it burning. Season to taste with salt and pepper.

Transfer the cheese ring to a warmed serving plate and spoon the ratatouille filling into the centre. Sprinkle with parsley and serve.

## Serves 6

# Red Pepper Macaroni Cheese

175 g (6 oz) wholewheat macaroni

**Sauce:**

25 g (1 oz) butter

25 g (1 oz) plain flour

750 ml (1¼ pints) milk

½ teaspoon English mustard

large pinch cayenne pepper

¼ teaspoon grated nutmeg

250 g (8 oz) Cheddar cheese, grated

1 red pepper, cored, deseeded and
  diced

2 tablespoons chopped parsley

**To garnish:**

oil, for shallow-frying

3 thin slices wholemeal bread, cut
  into 12 triangles

Cook the macaroni in lightly salted boiling water according to packet instructions. Drain and reserve.

Melt the butter in a large saucepan, add the flour and cook for 1 minute, stirring constantly. Gradually add the milk, stirring all the time. Bring the milk to the boil then simmer for 3 minutes. Add the mustard, cayenne and nutmeg. Stir in all but 25 g (1 oz) of the Cheddar. Season to taste with salt and pepper.

Plunge the diced pepper into boiling water. Bring the water back to the boil, then drain the pepper and add to the sauce with the macaroni. Reheat gently but thoroughly and stir in the parsley. Spoon into individual serving dishes or one large one. Sprinkle with the remaining Cheddar and brown under a preheated grill.

Meanwhile, heat the oil in a pan and fry the bread for a few seconds on each sides. Arrange the bread triangles around the macaroni.

## Serves 6

*right: gougere with ratatouille, red pepper macaroni cheese*

# Carrot and Apple Salad

375 g (12 oz) carrots, coarsely grated

3 Cox's Orange Pippins, cored and
   sliced

1 tablespoon lemon juice

1 tablespoon sunflower seeds

3 tablespoons raisins

2 teaspoons sunflower oil

2 tablespoons cashew nuts

150 ml (¼ pint) French dressing

little gem lettuce, to serve

Put the grated carrot into a large
bowl. Sprinkle the apple slices with
lemon juice to prevent them
discolouring and add them to the
bowl. Gently mix in the sunflower
seeds and raisins.

Heat the oil in a small pan and
lightly brown the cashew nuts.
Drain the nuts on kitchen paper
and leave to cool. Add the nuts to
the salad with the dressing and toss
gently to combine. Arrange the
outer leaves from the lettuce on a
serving plate and spoon the salad
into them.

**Serves 6**

# Hot Red Bean and Sweetcorn Salad

400 g (13 oz) can red kidney beans, rinsed and drained
200 g (7 oz) can sweetcorn, rinsed and drained
4 celery sticks, chopped
1 Spanish onion, thinly sliced
mustard and cress, to garnish

**Dressing:**
6 tablespoons olive oil
1 tablespoon white wine vinegar
½ teaspoon Tabasco sauce
½ teaspoon mustard powder
2 green chillies, cored, deseeded and finely chopped
salt and pepper

Put the beans, sweetcorn, celery and onion into a salad bowl.

To make the dressing, whisk together the oil, vinegar, Tabasco, mustard and chillies. Season with salt and pepper and pour over the bean mixture. Toss gently. Cover the salad and leave to stand for 1–2 hours. Serve sprinkled with mustard and cress.

**Serves 6**

*left: carrot and apple salad*
*right: orange winter salad*

# Orange Winter Salad

4 large oranges
400 g (13 oz) can red kidney beans, rinsed and drained
300 g (10 oz) bean sprouts
4 celery sticks, thinly sliced
watercress sprigs, to garnish

**Dressing:**
5 tablespoons olive oil
2 tablespoons lemon juice
¼ teaspoon sugar
¼ teaspoon mustard
salt and pepper

Cut the skin and white pith from the oranges. Cut the oranges into segments and put them into a bowl with any juice from them. Add the beans and bean sprouts with the celery and toss gently.

To make the dressing, whisk the oil and lemon juice, then add the sugar, mustard and salt and pepper to taste. Pour the dressing over the salad and toss gently. Garnish with watercress and serve.

**Serves 6**

# Lunches and Snacks

## Toasted Ham and Cheese Sandwich

1 slice of white bread
1 slice of wholemeal bread
softened butter, for spreading
50 g (2 oz) Cheddar cheese, grated
1 slice of ham, trimmed of fat
tomato wedges, to serve

Spread both slices of bread with some of the butter. Put one slice of bread, butter side down, on a grill rack. Sprinkle half the grated Cheddar on the bread. Sit the slice of ham on top and scatter with the remaining Cheddar.

Set the second slice of bread on the grated cheese, buttered side up. Press the sandwich gently together. Cook under a preheated grill for about 4 minutes, turning once.

Serve the golden sandwich cut into quarters and garnished with tomato wedges.

**Serves 1**

## Stripy Cheese Twists

125 g (4 oz) plain flour
pinch of mustard powder
50 g (2 oz) butter
50 g (2 oz) Cheddar cheese, finely grated
4 teaspoons cold water
1–2 tablespoons yeast extract

Sift the flour and mustard powder into a bowl. Rub in the butter and stir in the cheese. Add the water and mix to a soft but not sticky dough.

Lightly knead the dough on a floured work surface then roll it to a rectangle measuring about 25 x 15 cm (10 x 6 inches). Spread the yeast extract over the surface and fold the dough in half. Roll the dough again gently and cut it into 12 strips. Cut each strip in half and twist.

Arrange the cheese twists on greased baking sheets and bake in a preheated oven, 190°C (375°F), Gas Mark 5, for 10–12 minutes or until pale golden. Leave to cool on the baking sheet then transfer to a wire rack to cool completely.

**Makes 24**

## Chunky Chicken Soup

2 slices of wholemeal or granary bread
25 g (1 oz) Edam cheese, grated
425 g (14 oz) can cream of chicken soup
200 g (7 oz) can sweetcorn, rinsed and drained
4 mushrooms, finely sliced
50 g (2 oz) frozen peas
2 tablespoons milk

Toast the bread on one side only until golden. Turn the bread over and sprinkle with the grated cheese, put it under the grill and toast until the cheese is bubbling and melted. Leave to cool. Cut the cheese toasts into small squares and wrap them in foil if you want to keep them warm.

Pour the soup into a saucepan and add the sweetcorn, mushrooms, peas and milk. Heat gently for about 10 minutes, stirring occasionally, until all the vegetables are cooked through.

**Serves 2**

# Tomato and Courgette Soup

2 tablespoons olive oil

2 garlic cloves, halved

1 onion, chopped

750 g (1½ lb) ripe tomatoes, skinned, deseeded and chopped

750 ml (1¼ pints) vegetable stock

1 tablespoon tomato purée

2 courgettes, coarsely shredded

1 tablespoon chopped basil

salt and pepper

natural yogurt, to serve

basil leaves, to garnish

Heat the oil in a large saucepan, add the garlic and cook until golden then remove the garlic with a slotted spoon and discard. Add the onion to the pan with the tomatoes and cook gently for 2–3 minutes, stirring frequently.

Add the stock, tomato purée and corugettes to the pan. Bring to the boil and simmer for 10–15 minutes. Stir in the basil and season with salt and pepper. Serve the soup with a spoonful of natural yogurt and garnish with basil leaves.

## Serves 6

*above: tomato and courgette soup*

# Burger Brunch

4 beefburgers
2 burger buns
4 tablespoons tomato chutney
250 g (8 oz) mashed potato
125 g (4 oz) Cheddar cheese, grated
salt and pepper

Cook the burgers under a preheated, moderate grill for about 4 minutes on each side, or until cooked through. Split the burger buns in half and toast the cut surfaces lightly.

Spread the tomato chutney on the 4 cut sides of the buns and top each one with a grilled burger.

Divide the mashed potato into 4 portions and put 1 portion on top of each burger. Sprinkle with the grated Cheddar and bake in a preheated oven, 190°C (375°F), Gas Mark 5, for about 15 minutes or until the potato and cheese topping is golden. Serve the burgers immediately, with a green salad, if liked.

**Serves 4**

# Seaside Salad

125 g (4 oz) pasta shells
1 teaspoon sunflower oil
75 g (3 oz) canned tuna
2 celery sticks, trimmed and sliced
5 cm (2 inch) piece of cucumber, diced
1 red apple, diced
**Dressing:**
2 tablespoons mayonnaise
2 tablespoons natural yogurt
2 teaspoons lemon juice
salt and pepper

Bring a saucepan of lightly salted water to the boil, then cook the pasta shells according to packet instructions, until tender. Drain thoroughly, then stir in the sunflower oil.

Carefully stir the tuna, celery, cucumber and apple into the pasta.

Put all the ingredients for the dressing in a bowl and whisk together. Spoon the dressing over the salad and stir gently, to combine.

**Serves 2**

# Quick Quiches

175 g (6 oz) shortcrust pastry
**Filling:**
2 rashers of rindless streaky bacon, chopped
1 egg
3 tablespoons milk
25 g (1 oz) Cheddar cheese, grated
salt and pepper

Roll out the pastry thinly on a lightly floured surface. Cut out rounds using a 7 cm (3 inch) round cutter and use the pastry to line 8 patty tins. Prick the pastry bases and chill for 5 minutes. Line the pastry with scrunched foil and bake in a preheated oven, 200°C (400°F), Gas Mark 6, for 5 minutes. Remove the foil and return the pastry cases to the oven for a further 3 minutes.

Meanwhile, make the filling. Cook the streaky bacon gently until the fat begins to run. When it is cooked through, drain it well. Whisk the egg and milk and season with salt and pepper.

Divide the bacon between the pastry cases and pour over the egg mixture. Scatter the cheese over the top and bake for about 15 minutes, or until the quiches are puffy and cooked through.

**Serves 8**

*right: chicken in pitta pockets*

# Chicken in Pitta Pockets

4 pitta breads
2 tablespoons sunflower oil
1 garlic clove, crushed
500 g (1 lb) boneless, skinless chicken
  breasts, cut into strips
2 tablespoons mild chilli sauce
salt and pepper

**To serve:**
1 onion, thinly sliced
1 little gem lettuce, shredded
2 ripe tomatoes, deseeded and diced

Put the pitta breads to warm in a preheated oven, 140°C (275°F), Gas Mark 1, while preparing the filling.

Heat the oil in a frying pan or wok. Add the garlic and chicken and stir-fry for about 5 minutes or until the chicken is cooked. Stir in the sauce, coating all the chicken strips thoroughly. Season with salt and pepper.

Cut a slit along one side of each pitta. Spoon in a little of the onion, lettuce and tomato, then the chicken. Serve garnished with the remaining salad.

**Serves 4**

# Cyclops Specials

2 slices of wholemeal bread
butter, for spreading
2 eggs
75 g (3 oz) Cheddar or Edam cheese,
　finely grated

Toast the bread on one side until golden. Turn the slices over and spread with butter. Separate the eggs, keeping the yolks separate and the whites together. Stiffly whisk the egg whites and fold in the grated cheese. Spoon the mixture on top of the buttered toast. Put the yolk into the centre of the egg white mixture.

Cook under the grill for about 3 minutes, or until the egg mixture and yolk are cooked.

**Serves 2**

# Biker's Bananas

4 large slices of white bread
8 teaspoons smooth peanut butter
4 small bananas
2 teaspoons fresh lemon juice

Trim the crusts from the bread. Flatten each slice of bread with a rolling pin and spread with peanut butter. Peel the bananas and brush with lemon juice. Lay a banana on each slice of bread and roll them up tightly.

**Serves 4**

# BMX Baps

50 g (2 oz) cream cheese
125 g (4 oz) Cheddar cheese, grated
1 small celery stick, trimmed and
　finely chopped
2.5 cm (1 inch) piece of cucumber,
　finely chopped
4 wholemeal baps
1 carrot, peeled

Beat the cheeses together and stir in the celery and cucumber. Split the baps and spread the cheese mixture on the bases. Coarsely grate the carrot and divide between the baps. Gently press on the tops. Wrap well.

**Serves 4**

*above:* cyclops specials

44

# Egg and Tuna Triple Deckers

90 g (3½ oz) can tuna, drained
1 tablespoon thick natural yogurt
1 tablespoon tomato ketchup
2 eggs, hard-boiled
1 tablespoon mayonnaise
8 slices of brown bread
4 slices of white bread
50 g (2 oz) butter, softened

Put the tuna, yogurt and tomato ketchup into a bowl and mix together. In a second bowl, mash the hard-boiled eggs and stir in the mayonnaise.

Spread 4 slices of brown bread and the white bread with butter. Spread the remaining 4 slices of brown bread with the egg mayonnaise mixture and the buttered white bread with the tuna mixture.

To assemble the tripled decker sandwiches, start with brown bread with egg mayonnaise, then make a layer with white bread with tuna mixture and top with buttered brown bread. Repeat with the remaining bread to make four sandwiches. Trim the crusts from the bread if liked. Cut the sandwiches into triangles.

**Serves 4**

# Buttons and Bows

125 g (4 oz) pasta bows
25 g (1 oz) plain flour
25 g (1 oz) butter
pinch of mustard powder
450 ml (¾ pint) milk
50 g (2 oz) frozen peas
50 g (2 oz) frozen sweetcorn
1 tomato, diced
90 g (3½ oz) can tuna, drained and flaked
125 g (4 oz) Gouda cheese, grated
25 g (1 oz) fresh brown breadcrumbs
salt and pepper

Bring a large pan of lightly salted water to the boil, add the pasta bows and cook according to packet instructions. Drain.

Put the flour, butter, mustard and milk into a saucepan and heat, stirring constantly, until the sauce boils and thickens. Reduce the heat and stir in the peas, sweetcorn, tomato and tuna. Cook for about 3 minutes. Stir in half the grated cheese.

Mix together the pasta and sauce and spoon into a heatproof serving dish. Mix the remaining cheese with the breadcrumbs and sprinkle it over the pasta mixture. Place the dish under a preheated grill for about 4 minutes or until the mixture is bubbling and the cheese has melted.

**Serves 4**

# Baked Potatoes with Mushrooms

2 large potatoes, each weighing about 250 g (8 oz)
**Filling:**
25 g (1 oz) butter
125 g (4 oz) button mushrooms, sliced
50 g (2 oz) cream cheese
4 teaspoons tomato relish

Scrub the potatoes and score around the middle lengthways. Place them on a baking sheet and bake in a preheated oven, 200°C (400°F), Gas Mark 6, for about 1 hour, or until they have cooked through.

Carefully cut the potatoes in half using the scored line as a guide. Scoop the potato flesh into a bowl, leaving a thin layer of potato near the skin. Mash the potato with the butter, mushrooms and cheese.

Spoon the potato mixture back into the shells and spoon the tomato relish on top. Arrange the potato shells on the baking sheet and return to the oven for about 10 minutes or until heated through.

**Serves 4**

# Jungleburgers

**Jungle:**

½ iceberg lettuce, shredded

4 slices of red pepper, halved

25 g (1 oz) fresh bean sprouts

4 small celery sticks with leaves

**Burgers:**

500 g (1 lb) good quality lean minced
   beef

½ teaspoon chopped basil

½ teaspoon chopped oregano

1 teaspoon chopped parsley

1 small onion, finely chopped

50 g (2 oz) fresh brown breadcrumbs

1 egg

2 teaspoons tomato relish

salt and pepper

First prepare the burgers. In a large bowl mix together the beef, herbs, onion and breadcrumbs. Season with salt and pepper. Beat the egg with the tomato relish and work it into the beef mixture. Divide into 8 pieces and shape into burgers. Grill the burgers for about 10 minutes, turning them after 5 minutes so they cook evenly.

Meanwhile, assemble the jungle. Divide the lettuce between 4 plates and arrange the red pepper (these resemble snakes), bean sprouts (logs) and celery (trees) on top. Put 2 burgers in the middle of each jungle and serve.

**Serves 4**

# Chicken and Egg Toasties

50 g (2 oz) butter

4 slices of white bread, crusts
   removed

3 eggs

3 tablespoons milk

125 g (4 oz) cooked chicken, chopped

½ red pepper, cored, deseeded and
   finely diced

2 spring onions, finely chopped

25 g (1 oz) Cheddar cheese, grated

salt and pepper

Melt half the butter and brush on both sides of the bread. Line 4 individual Yorkshire pudding tins with the bread slices, pressing them down but leaving the corners sticking up. Bake in a preheated oven, 200°C (400°F), Gas Mark 6, for about 15 minutes, until crisp and golden.

Meanwhile, whisk the eggs and milk and season with salt and pepper. Melt the remaining butter in a pan, add the egg mixture and stir over a gentle heat until the eggs have just cooked. Stir the chicken, pepper, onion and cheese into the egg mixture and divide between the crispy bread cases.

**Serves 4**

*left:* jungleburgers
*right:* cheese and raisin sandwiches,
tuna scramble rolls

# Cheese and Raisin Sandwiches

4 large slices of white bread
4 large slices of wholemeal bread
50 g (2 oz) butter, softened
**Filling:**
175 g (6 oz) Cheddar or Edam
  cheese, grated
25 g (1 oz) seedless raisins, washed
  and dried
1 tablespoon mayonnaise

Spread the bread with the butter.

Mix together the cheese, raisins and mayonnaise and spread over the white bread slices. Cover with the wholemeal bread slices. Press down firmly and cut into quarters, then remove the crusts, if liked.

**Serves 4**

# Tuna Scramble Rolls

200 g (7 oz) can tuna, drained
1 tablespoon fresh lemon juice
1 tablespoon chopped parsley
4 eggs
50 g (2 oz) butter, softened
4 granary rolls
salt and pepper

Mash the tuna in a bowl with the lemon juice and season to taste with salt and pepper. Stir in the parsley.

Beat the eggs in a bowl and season with salt and pepper. Melt half the butter in a small saucepan, add the beaten egg and stir over a gentle heat until the eggs have just cooked. Leave to cool.

Split the rolls and spread them with the remaining butter. Spread the tuna mixture over the bottom half of each roll. Add the scrambled egg and cover with the tops.

**Serves 4**

# Cream Cheese and Pineapple Sandwiches

4 large slices of granary bread
2 tablespoons mango chutney
125 g (4 oz) cream cheese
50 g (2 oz) sliced pineapple, chopped
salt and pepper

Spread the bread with the chutney. Beat together the cream cheese and pineapple and season with salt and pepper. Spread the cream cheese mixture over the bread. Trim the crusts from the bread and roll up the bread like a Swiss roll. When you are ready to serve, cut each roll into 4 pieces.

**Serves 4**

# Totem Rolls

4 long, seeded bread rolls
6 slices of processed cheese
4 small slices of lean ham
25 g (1 oz) butter, softened
2 teaspoons chopped marjoram

Carefully cut each roll lengthways into 2 slices, cutting not quite all the way through. Divide 4 slices of cheese and the ham between the cut rolls, tucking the ham around the cheese. Spread the butter over the top of each filled roll. Cut the remaining cheese into thin strips and arrange them across each roll to resemble totem pole patterns. Sprinkle with marjoram.

Sit the rolls in foil boats and bake in a preheated oven, 200°C (400°F), Gas Mark 6, for about 10 minutes, or until the cheese is just beginning to melt.

**Serves 4**

# Parmesan Chicken Drumsticks

25 g (1 oz) fresh white breadcrumbs
25 g (1 oz) Parmesan cheese, grated
1 tablespoon plain flour
4 chicken drumsticks, skinned
1 egg, beaten
salt and pepper

Mix together the breadcrumbs and cheese. Season the flour with salt and pepper and dust over the drumsticks. Dip the drumsticks into the beaten egg then roll them in the breadcrumb mixture. When they are thoroughly coated chill them for about 15 minutes.

Cook the drumsticks under a preheated grill for about 25 minutes, turning them frequently until they are golden and cooked through.

**Serves 4**

# Cheesy Scotch Eggs

500 g (1 lb) mashed potatoes
125 g (4 oz) Cheddar cheese, grated
4 hard-boiled eggs, shelled
1 egg, beaten
50 g (2 oz) fine breadcrumbs
sunflower oil, for deep frying
salt and pepper

Beat the mashed potato and cheese and season with salt and pepper. Using floured hands, divide the mixture into 4 and mould around each egg.

Dip the coated eggs in the beaten egg and coat in the breadcrumbs.

Heat the oil in a deep-fryer or large saucepan and fry the eggs for 5 minutes, or until golden all over. Drain the Scotch eggs on kitchen paper and leave to cool.

**Serves 4**

*right: cheesy Scotch eggs*

# Cornish Pasties

250 g (8 oz) shortcrust pastry
**Filling:**
175 g (6 oz) cooked beef, thinly
   sliced
250 g (8 oz) potato, grated
1 onion, grated
15 g (½ oz) butter, diced
1 egg yolk
salt and pepper

First prepare the filling: Mix together the meat, potato and onion and season to taste with salt and pepper.

Roll out the pastry on a lightly floured surface and cut out four 15 cm (6 inch) rounds. Spoon the filling into the pastry rounds to within 1 cm (½ inch) of the rims. Top each portion with diced butter. Dampen the pastry edges with water and pinch together to seal well, forming a fluted edge. Make a small slit in the side of each pasty.

Brush each pasty with egg yolk, arrange on a baking sheet and bake in a preheated oven, 200°C (400°F), Gas Mark 6, for 10 minutes then reduce the temperature to 180°C (350°F), Gas Mark 4 and cook for a further 25 minutes or until golden brown. Serve warm or cold.

**Serves 4**

# French Bread Pizza with Bacon

250 g (8 oz) rashers of rindless back bacon
1 French stick
3 tablespoons tomato purée
200 g (7 oz) can chopped tomatoes, drained
1 tablespoon finely chopped oregano
125 g (4 oz) Cheddar cheese, grated
salt and pepper

Cook the bacon under a preheated grill for about 10 minutes until crisp. Leave to cool then crumble coarsely.

Cut the French stick in half and slice each half horizontally. Place the 4 pieces under the grill and toast the cut sides until golden. Spread the tomato purée evenly over the toasted bread and place the tomatoes on top. Sprinkle over the crumbled bacon and oregano. Season to taste with salt and pepper and sprinkle the grated cheese on top. Return the bread to the grill and cook for 10 minutes, until golden and bubbling. Serve immediately, cut into slices.

**Serves 6**

# Waldorf Salad

2 tablespoons fresh lemon juice
1 teaspoon caster sugar
150 ml (¼ pint) mayonnaise
500 g (1 lb) red dessert apples, cored
½ head celery, trimmed and chopped
50 g (2 oz) walnut pieces, chopped
1 lettuce, divided into leaves

Mix together the lemon juice, sugar and 1 tablespoon of the mayonnaise. Slice 1 apple thinly and chop the rest. Dip the apple slices in the mayonnaise dressing and set aside. Add the diced apple to the remaining dressing, turn to coat thoroughly, then cover and set aside for 30 minutes.

Add the celery and walnuts to the diced apple with the remaining mayonnaise and stir well to mix. Line a large rigid container with the lettuce leaves, pile the salad in the centre and arrange the apple slices on top.

**Serves 6**

*left:* cornish pasties
*right:* Waldorf salad

# Desserts

## Fruit and Yogurt Jelly

50 ml (2 fl oz) water
15 g (½ oz) powdered gelatine
250 g (8 oz) Greek-style yogurt
300 g (10 oz) can strawberries in
   natural juice, sieved
300 ml (½ pint) Caribbean-style fruit
   juice

Bring the water to the boil and
whisk in the gelatine until it has
dissolved. Put the yogurt into a jug
with the strawberries and their juice
and pour in enough of the fruit
juice to make the liquid up to
600 ml (1 pint). Quickly stir in the
dissolved gelatine.

Pour the jelly into 4 individual
150 ml (¼ pint) moulds or into a
600 ml (1 pint) serving dish. Chill
for about 4 hours or until set.

To serve, quickly dip the base of
the moulds in hot water then turn
them out on to individual dessert
plates or 1 large serving plate.

**Serves 4**

## Fresh Orange Jelly

150 ml (5 fl oz) fresh orange juice
½ teaspoon powdered gelatine
1 orange, skin and pith removed
thinly pared orange rind, to decorate

Heat the orange juice in a saucepan
until it is just beginning to boil.
Remove the pan from the heat and
whisk in the gelatine. When the
gelatine has dissolved completely,
leave it to cool.

When the orange jelly is
beginning to set, coarsely chop the
orange flesh and divide it between
2 pretty glasses. Pour the nearly set
jelly over the fruit and chill until set
completely. Serve decorated with
shredded orange rind.

**Serves 2**

## Blackcurrant Sorbet

500 g (1 lb) blackcurrants
2 tablespoons blackcurrant syrup
125 g (4 oz) granulated sugar
150 ml (¼ pint) water
juice of ½ lemon
1 egg white
dessert biscuits, to serve

Simmer the blackcurrants in a
saucepan with the syrup until soft.
Purée in a food processor then sieve
to remove the pips.

Heat the sugar and water in a
saucepan until the sugar has
dissolved. Increase the heat and boil
for about 5 minutes or until syrupy.
Leave to cool.

Mix the blackcurrant purée with
the sugar syrup in a rigid container
then add the lemon juice. Freeze for
about 2 hours, or until slushy.

Remove the blackcurrant mixture
from the freezer and beat until well
mixed. Whisk the egg white until
stiff then fold it into the
blackcurrant mixture. Return to the
freezer until solid.

Remove the sorbet from the
freezer about 10 minutes before
serving to soften a little. Serve with
dessert biscuits.

**Serves 4**

# Butterscotch Ice Cream

125 g (4 oz) soft dark brown sugar

150 ml (¼ pint) water

25 g (1 oz) butter

2 teaspoons lemon juice

2 teaspoons arrowroot, blended with
   2 teaspoons water

410 g (13½ oz) can evaporated milk,
   chilled overnight

3 drops vanilla extract

dessert biscuits, to serve

Dissolve the sugar in the water over a low heat. Add the butter and lemon juice and cook rapidly, without stirring, for about 5 minutes. Stir in the arrowroot mixture then reduce the heat, and simmer until the butterscotch has thickened. Leave to cool.

Pour the evaporated milk into a bowl, and whisk until thick and frothy. Fold in the cold butterscotch mixture and vanilla extract. Pour the mixture into a freezer container and freeze for 2 hours.

Beat the butterscotch mixture

again then return it to the freezer until you are ready to serve.

Remove the ice cream from the freezer 10 minutes before serving to soften a little. Serve with dessert biscuits.

## Serves 6

*above: blackcurrant sorbet, butterscotch ice cream*

# Igloo Puddings

250 g (8 oz) can pineapple rings in
  natural juice, drained
12 small seedless grapes
2 egg whites
125 g (4 oz) caster sugar
1 small Arctic roll

Line a baking sheet with foil.
Arrange 4 pineapple rings on the
foil and put 3 grapes into each ring.
Whisk the egg whites in a bowl
until stiff but not dry, then
gradually whisk in the sugar.

Cut the Arctic roll into 4 and put
a slice on top of each pineapple
ring, pressing it down with the back
of a spoon. Swirl the meringue over
the Arctic roll and pineapple, to
cover completely. Cook the
puddings under a preheated grill
until the meringue is very lightly
browned.

**Serves 4**

# Banana Whip

4 bananas
1 tablespoon lemon juice
1 egg white
50 g (2 oz) soft light brown sugar
150 ml (¼ pint) double cream
plain chocolate curls, to decorate

Mash the bananas with the lemon
juice. Whisk the egg white until stiff
and gradually whisk in the sugar.
Fold the banana purée into the
meringue mixture. Divide between
6 individual freezerproof dishes and
freeze for about 2 hours.

Remove the banana whips from
the freezer about 10 minutes before
serving to soften a little. Serve
decorated with chocolate curls.

**Serves 6**

# Indian Apples

4 medium cooking apples, cored
4 glacé cherries
25 g (1 oz) raisins, chopped
15 g (½ oz) dates, chopped
15 g (½ oz) walnuts, chopped
3 tablespoons clear honey
juice of 2 oranges

Score the apples around the middle
and arrange in an ovenproof dish.
Push a glacé cherry down through
the hole in each of the apples. Mix
together the raisins, dates and
walnuts in a bowl and stir in
1 tablespoon of the honey. Spoon
the mixed fruits on top of the
cherry. Drizzle the remaining honey
over the apples and pour over the
orange juice.

Bake the apples in a preheated
oven, 180°C (350°F), Gas Mark 4,
for about 40 minutes, basting them
occasionally with the juices in the
dish. Leave the apples to stand for
about 10 minutes before serving.

**Serves 4**

*left:* igloo puddings
*right:* sci-fi trifle

# Sci-fi Trifle

**125 g (4 oz) sponge fingers**

**410 g (13½ oz) can loganberries in natural juice**

**142 g (5 oz) packet raspberry jelly, torn into cubes**

**410 g (13½ oz) can evaporated milk, chilled overnight**

**150 ml (¼ pint) double cream**

**tube of sugar coated chocolate beans**

Set aside 8 of the sponge fingers. Arrange the remainder in a glass serving bowl. Drain the loganberries over a bowl. Sprinkle 4 tablespoons of the loganberry juice over the sponge fingers in the bowl and pour the rest into the measuring jug. Add enough water to make the liquid up to 300 ml (½ pint). Pour the loganberry juice into a saucepan, add the jelly and heat gently until melted. Remove from the heat and leave to cool.

Whisk the evaporated milk until thick. This will take about 15 minutes. Gradually whisk in the jelly mixture, whisking until frothy and thickened. Scatter the loganberries over the sponge fingers and pour over the jelly mixture. Chill for about 3 hours or until set.

Lightly whip the cream and spoon it into the centre of the jelly to resemble a dome. Arrange the sponge fingers radiating from the cream to the edge of the dish and sit the sugar covered beans over the jelly to resemble space ship portholes.

**Serves 10**

# Cheesecake Crown

75 g (3 oz) butter, melted

175 g (6 oz) muesli cookies, crushed

135 g (4½ oz) packet blackcurrant jelly, torn into cubes

150 g (5 oz) carton blackcurrant yogurt

250 g (8 oz) cream cheese

1 egg white

14 rectangular ice cream wafers

240 g (7½ oz) tube white icing

jelly tot sweets, to decorate

Stir together the melted butter and crushed cookies and press into a 15cm (6 inch) deep round loose-based cake tin.

Put the jelly into a measuring jug and add enough boiling water to make 150 ml (¼ pint). Stir the jelly until it has melted. Leave to cool.

Stir the yogurt and cream cheese until smooth, then beat in the cooled jelly.

Whisk the egg white until stiff then carefully fold it into the blackcurrant mixture. Pour the blackcurrant mixture over the biscuit base and level the surface.

Chill for about 4 hours, or until set.

Run a warm palette knife around the edge of the tin to loosen the cheesecake, then turn it out on to a serving plate.

Trim the wafers to a point and arrange them around the cake to make a crown, pressing them on to the sides with a little white icing. Pipe small blobs of icing on to the wafers and stick a jelly sweet on top to make jewels.

**Serves 8**

# Fresh Fruit Salad

1 ogen melon

2 oranges, peeled and segmented

2 apples, cored and sliced

2 pears, peeled, cored and chopped

125 g (4 oz) seedless grapes

½ yellow-fleshed grapefruit, peeled
   and segmented

½ pink-fleshed grapefruit, peeled and
   segmented

1 kiwi fruit, peeled and sliced

250 g (8 oz) strawberries, hulled and
   halved

1–2 tablespoons clear honey

juice of 1 lemon

Greek-style yogurt, to serve

Cut the melon in half and discard the seeds. Scoop out the flesh with a melon baller. Mix together all the fruits and spoon them into a serving dish. Stir the honey with the lemon juice and pour over the fruit. Serve as soon as possible with the yogurt.

**Serves 6**

# Raspberry Banana Boats

250 g (8 oz) raspberries, thawed if
  frozen
2 tablespoons icing sugar, sifted
150 ml (¼ pint) double cream
4 bananas
300 ml (½ pint) vanilla ice cream
coloured sugar crystals, to decorate

Reserve a few of the raspberries for decoration. Press the remaining berries through a sieve and stir in the icing sugar until dissolved. Mix the raspberry purée with half of the cream and lightly whip the remaining cream.

Halve the bananas lengthways and arrange two halves in each of 4 individual shallow serving dishes. Top each serving with a scoop of ice cream, then drizzle over the raspberry cream. Spoon the lightly whipped cream on top and sprinkle with coloured sugar crystals. Add the reserved raspberries and serve.

**Serves 4**

# Orange and Yogurt Mould

thinly pared rind and juice of 4 large
  oranges
about 150 ml (¼ pint) water
125 g (4 oz) caster sugar
15 g (½ oz) powdered gelatine
3 tablespoons fresh lemon juice
150 g (5 oz) carton natural yogurt

Squeeze the orange juice into a measuring jug and make up the juice to 300 ml (½ pint) with water if necessary. Stir the juice into a saucepan with the orange rind, the water and sugar and heat gently until the sugar has dissolved. Bring to the boil slowly, then remove from the heat and leave to stand for 5 minutes.

Strain the juice through a sieve then whisk in the gelatine until it has dissolved. Add the lemon juice. Leave the mixture to stand until it is almost set then fold in the yogurt. Pour the mixture into a mould then chill for about 4 hours or until firm.

To serve, quickly dip the base of the mould in hot water then turn out on to a serving plate.

**Serves 6**

*left: raspberry banana boats*
*right: orange and yogurt mould, ice
cream crunch*

# Ice Cream Crunch

4 egg yolks

125 g (4 oz) caster sugar

1 tablespoon cornflour

450 ml (¾ pint) milk

few drops vanilla extract

50 g (2 oz) dried wholemeal
   breadcrumbs

150 ml (¼ pint) double cream

Beat the egg yolks with 75 g (3 oz) of the sugar and the cornflour until pale and creamy. Heat the milk until it is just beginning to bubble, then pour it over the egg mixture, whisking continuously. Stir in the vanilla extract.

Pour the mixture into the rinsed pan and cook over a gentle heat, stirring frequently, until the custard has thickened and coats the back of the spoon. Remove from the heat and whisk until cool. Pour into a freezer container and freeze for about 1 hour, until beginning to freeze around the edges.

Meanwhile, mix the breadcrumbs with the remaining sugar and cook them under a preheated, moderate grill until lightly toasted. Leave to cool. Lightly whip the cream and fold it into the frozen custard with the breadcrumb mixture. Return the custard to the freezer and freeze for 1 hour.

Beat the mixture again then return to the freezer until ready to serve. Remove the ice cream from the freezer 10 minutes before serving to soften a little.

**Serves 6**

# Orange and Banana Pudding

125 g (4 oz) butter, softened
125 g (4 oz) soft light brown sugar
2 eggs, beaten
125 g (4 oz) self-raising flour
1 teaspoon baking powder
15 g (½ oz) cocoa powder
grated rind and juice of 1 orange
2 ripe bananas, sliced
**To decorate:**
1 ripe banana, sliced and sprinkled
 with lemon juice
fine strands of orange rind

Cream the butter and sugar then gradually beat in the eggs. Sift the flour, baking powder and cocoa powder over the creamed mixture, and fold in with the orange rind and juice. Carefully stir in the sliced bananas. Spoon the mixture into a buttered 900 ml (1½ pint) pudding basin. Cover the basin with pleated greaseproof paper and foil and tie securely with string.

Steam the pudding for 2 hours, topping up the steamer with boiling water as necessary.

Turn the pudding on to a warmed serving plate and decorate with slices of banana and orange rind. Serve with custard or chocolate sauce.

**Serves 6**

# Hot Chocolate Trifle

410 g (13½ oz) can apricot halves in
 natural juice
1 chocolate Swiss roll, sliced
2 tablespoons custard powder
2 eggs, separated
1 tablespoon drinking chocolate
1 teaspoon cocoa powder
2 teaspoons granulated sugar
600 ml (1 pint) milk
125 g (4 oz) caster sugar

Drain the apricots, reserving the juice. Arrange the Swiss roll and apricots in a 1.2 litre (2 pint) ovenproof dish and spoon some of the reserved fruit juice over the top.

Mix the custard powder, egg yolks, drinking chocolate, cocoa powder and sugar with a little milk until it forms a paste. Pour the remaining milk into a saucepan and heat until it begins to bubble, then pour it over the custard mixture. Wash the pan and return the liquid to it. Stir over a gentle heat for 2 minutes, until thickened, then pour over the apricot mixture.

Whisk the egg whites until stiff then whisk in the caster sugar. Spoon the meringue over the chocolate custard and swirl into soft peaks. Bake in a preheated oven, 180°C (350°F), Gas Mark 4, for 20 minutes or until the meringue is golden. Serve the trifle hot or warm.

**Serves 6**

# Loch Ness Monster

500 g (1 lb) fresh or frozen
 blackberries or raspberries
1 teaspoon arrowroot
4 tablespoons orange juice
3 large bananas
6 fine chocolate orange sticks, broken
 into 1 cm (½ inch) pieces
2 raisins
4 scoops vanilla ice cream

Put the blackberries or raspberries into a saucepan. Whisk together the arrowroot and orange juice, pour over the fruit and heat gently until the mixture just begins to bubble. Remove from the heat and leave to cool.

Cut the bananas to resemble the body, neck and head of the monster. Press the pieces of chocolate into the banana to make spikes. Press the raisins into the side of the head to resemble eyes.

Spoon the cooled fruit mixture into a serving dish and arrange the banana pieces to form the monster. Add the ice cream to the dish to look like rocks.

**Serves 4**

*right: hot chocolate trifle*

# Chocolate Bread and Butter Pudding

6 slices of fruit bread

40 g (1½ oz) butter, softened

40 g (1½ oz) chocolate and hazelnut spread

600 ml (1 pint) milk

25 g (1 oz) drinking chocolate

25 g (1 oz) caster sugar

2 eggs

Spread the fruit bread with the butter and the chocolate and hazelnut spread. Cut the bread into triangles and arrange them in a buttered 1.2 litre (2 pint) ovenproof dish.

Heat about one-third of the milk in a saucepan, then whisk in the drinking chocolate and sugar. Leave to cool.

Beat the eggs with the remaining milk and stir in the chocolate flavoured milk. Strain the flavoured milk over the bread and leave it to stand for 30 minutes. Bake the pudding in a preheated oven, 160°C (325°F), Gas Mark 3, for about 45 minutes or until it is set and crisp on top. Serve immediately, with cream or custard, if liked.

## Serves 4–5

# Chocolate Ice Cream

2 eggs, separated
65 ml (2½ fl oz) double cream
50 g (2 oz) caster sugar
175 g (6 oz) can evaporated milk,
  chilled overnight
125 g (4 oz) plain chocolate, melted
fresh fruit or dessert biscuits, to serve

Beat together the egg yolks and
double cream. Whisk the egg whites
until stiff then gradually whisk in
the sugar. Fold the cream and
meringue mixture together. Whisk
the chilled evaporated milk until
thick and frothy, fold in the egg
mixture and the melted chocolate.
Pour into a rigid container and
freeze for 2 hours until slushy.

  Beat the ice cream until smooth
then freeze until firm.

  Remove the ice cream from the
freezer 10 minutes before serving to
soften a little. Serve with fresh fruit
or dessert biscuits.

## Serves 6

*left chocolate bread and butter
pudding*
*right: yogurt knickerbocker glory*

# Yogurt Knickerbocker Glory

2 large bananas, sliced
1 tablespoon fresh lemon juice
250 g (8 oz) carton thick Greek-style
  yogurt
300 ml (½ pint) raspberry yogurt
chopped almonds, to decorate

Dip the sliced bananas into the
lemon juice to stop them
discolouring, reserve a few for
decoration. Using 4 tall glasses,
make layers of Greek yogurt,
raspberry yogurt and sliced banana.
Finish with a layer of yogurt, then
decorate with banana slices and
chopped almonds.

## Serves 4

# Banana and Chocolate Pancakes

125 g (4 oz) plain flour
pinch of salt
1 egg, beaten
300 ml (½ pint) milk and water mixed
oil, for frying
**Filling:**
2 large bananas
125 g (4 oz) curd cheese
150 g (5 oz) carton chocolate yogurt

**To serve:**
1 banana, sliced diagonally
fresh chocolate sauce

Sift the flour and salt into a mixing bowl and make a well in the centre. Add the egg and half the milk mixture. Beat until smooth, then gradually stir in the remaining milk. Pour the batter into a jug and leave to stand for 25 minutes.

Wipe an 18 cm (7 inch) non-stick pancake pan with a little oil. Heat the pan then pour a thin layer of batter over the base. Cook until the underside is golden then flip over and cook until golden on the other side. Turn on to a warmed plate and continue with the remaining batter. You will make about 12 pancakes.

Mash the bananas with a fork. Stir in the curd cheese and yogurt. Divide the mixture between the pancakes and roll them up. Arrange two pancakes on each plate and decorate with the sliced banana. Pour over a little chocolate sauce and serve the rest separately.

**Serves 6**

# Real American Ice Cream

175 ml (6 fl oz) milk
300 ml (½ pint) single cream
1 vanilla pod, split
4 egg yolks
125 g (4 oz) caster sugar
pinch of salt
**Fudge sauce:**
25 g (1 oz) cocoa powder
75 g (3 oz) caster sugar
150 g (5 oz) golden syrup
25 ml (1 fl oz) water
150 ml (5 fl oz) single cream
125 g (4 oz) butter
1 teaspoon vanilla extract

Heat the milk, cream and vanilla pod in a saucepan until just beginning to steam. Whisk the egg yolks with the sugar and salt until thick. Stir in about 4 tablespoons of the hot milk and mix well then pour back into the pan. Remove the vanilla pod. Gently heat the mixture, stirring continuously, until the mixture thickens; this will take about 10 minutes – the mixture should be thick enough to coat the back of the spoon. Leave to cool.

Beat the ice cream mixture well then pour it into a rigid container and freeze for about 2 hours.

Whisk the ice cream until smooth, then return it to the freezer and freeze until firm.

Remove the ice cream from the freezer about 10 minutes before serving to soften a little.

Make the fudge sauce when you are ready to serve: Put the cocoa powder, sugar, syrup, water, cream and butter into a saucepan and heat gently until the mixture is smooth. Increase the heat and simmer for about 5 minutes, until the mixture begins to thicken. Leave to cool for about 5 minutes then serve with the ice cream.

**Serves 6**

*left: banana and chocolate pancakes*
*above: real American ice cream*

# Fruity Fools

425 g (14 oz) can apricot halves in natural juice, drained
150 g (5 oz) carton mandarin yogurt
150 ml (¼ pint) fresh custard
chocolate flakes, crumbled, to decorate

Purée the apricots in a food processor or liquidizer. Stir together the apricot purée, yogurt and custard. Divide the fool between 4 dessert glasses and sprinkle with the flaked chocolate.

**Serves 4**

# Strawberry Shortcake

125 g (4 oz) butter
50 g (2 oz) caster sugar
125 g (4 oz) plain flour, sieved
50 g (2 oz) cornflour, sifted
250 g (8 oz) strawberries
300 ml (½ pint) double cream,
    whipped
icing sugar, for dusting

Cream the butter and sugar until
soft and fluffy, then stir in the flour
and cornflour. Mix to a firm dough,
then turn on to a floured surface
and knead lightly.

Divide the mixture in half and
roll each piece into a 20 cm (8 inch)
round on a baking tray. Bake in a
preheated oven, 180°C (350°F), Gas
Mark 4, for 20 minutes. Leave for a
few minutes, then mark one round
into 6 sections. Carefully slide both
rounds on to a wire rack to cool.

Slice the strawberries lengthways.
Set aside six slices for decoration.
Mix three-quarters of the cream
with the strawberries and spread
over the plain round of shortcake.
Break the other round into six
sections and place on top. Sprinkle
with icing sugar. Pipe a cream
rosette on each section and decorate
with the reserved strawberry slices.

**Serves 6**

# Deep Dish Apple Pie

250 g (8 oz) sweet shortcrust pastry
875 g (1¾ lb) tart cooking apples,
    peeled, cored and thinly sliced
125 g (4 oz) caster sugar
½ teaspoon ground cinnamon
25 g (1 oz) butter, finely diced
a little egg white
caster sugar, for sprinkling

Roll out the pastry on a lightly
floured surface to a 30 cm (12 inch)
round. Trim a 2.5 cm (1 inch) strip
around the edge and use this strip
to line the rim of a 20 cm (8 inch)
pie dish. Toss the apples with the
caster sugar, cinnamon and butter
and pack into the pie dish. Dampen
the rim of pastry with a little water
and set the pastry circle on top of
the pie to form a lid. Pinch the
edges together and flute to decorate.
Brush the top of the pastry with egg
white and sprinkle with caster sugar.

Bake the pie in a preheated oven,
230°C (450°F), Gas Mark 8, for
15 minutes, then reduce the oven
temperature to 180°C (350°F), Gas
Mark 4 and bake for a further
35 minutes, until the pastry is
golden and the apple is tender.
Serve the pie with custard or vanilla
ice cream.

## Serves 6

*left:* deep dish apple pie
*right:* steamed chocolate pudding

# Steamed Chocolate Pudding

125 g (4 oz) butter, softened

125 g (4 oz) soft light brown sugar

2 eggs, beaten

3 tablespoons milk

175 g (6 oz) self-raising flour

2 tablespoons cocoa powder

2 teaspoons baking powder

**Chocolate sauce:**

125 g (4 oz) plain chocolate, chopped

25 g (1 oz) soft light brown sugar

2 tablespoons water

Cream the butter and sugar in a bowl until pale and light. Gradually beat in the eggs and milk. Sift the flour, cocoa powder and baking powder and fold into the creamed mixture. Spoon into a greased 1.2 litre (2 pint) pudding basin. Cover with pleated greaseproof paper and foil. Tie securely and steam for 2 hours – topping up the steamer with boiling water as necessary.

Meanwhile, make the sauce. Put the chocolate, sugar and water into a small pan and heat until the sugar and chocolate have melted.

To serve, turn the chocolate pudding on to a warmed serving plate and pour over the sauce.

**Serves 6**

# Baked Alaska

2 eggs
75 g (3 oz) caster sugar
50 g (2 oz) plain flour, sifted
4 tablespoons orange juice
3 nectarines
600 ml (1 pint) vanilla ice cream
**Meringue:**
4 egg whites
250 g (8 oz) caster sugar

Whisk the eggs and caster sugar in a bowl until a ribbon-like trail is left when the whisks are lifted. Sift the flour over the mixture and fold it in using a metal spoon. Spoon the mixture into a greased and base-lined 20 cm (8 inch) sandwich tin. Bake in a preheated oven, 180°C (350°F), Gas Mark 4, for about 20 minutes or until risen and golden. Turn the sponge on to a wire rack, discard the lining paper and leave to cool.

Put the sponge on an ovenproof serving plate and sprinkle with 3 tablespoons of the orange juice. Stone and thinly slice the nectarines and arrange them on top of the sponge. Scoop the ice cream on top and put the plate in the freezer.

Whisk the egg whites until stiff then gradually whisk in the caster sugar. Swirl the meringue over the sponge fruit and ice cream, to cover completely. Bake in a preheated oven, 220°C (425°F), Gas Mark 7, for 8–10 minutes, or until the meringue is lightly browned. If you are serving the alaska for a special occasion, set sparklers alight and stand them in the dessert.

**Serves 8**

# Mango Mousse

3 large ripe mangoes, peeled and
   stoned
1–2 tablespoons lime juice
300 ml (½ pint) double cream
orange or mandarin segments, to
   decorate

Put the mango flesh into a food processor or blender with half the lime juice and blend to a purée. Lightly whip the cream and fold in the mango pulp; taste the mixture and add more lime juice if necessary. Spoon the mousse into a rigid container, then cover and freeze for 1 hour.

Beat the mousse until smooth and return it to the freezer for 1 further hour. Serve the mousse in individual bowls and decorate with orange or mandarin segments.

**Serves 8**

*left:* baked Alaska
*right:* mango mousse

# Cakes and Bakes

## Chocolate and Oat Bars

125 ml (4 fl oz) sunflower oil
1 tablespoon clear honey
25 g (1 oz) demerara sugar
125 g (4 oz) porridge oats
125 g (4 oz) wholemeal flour
75 g (3 oz) milk chocolate, melted

Grease and base-line an 18 cm (7 inch) shallow square tin. Stir together the oil, honey, sugar, oats and flour and press half the mixture into the prepared tin. Pour the melted chocolate over the mixture and spread evenly. Spoon over the remaining oat mixture and press gently and evenly. Bake in a preheated oven, 190°C (375°F), Gas Mark 5, for 20–25 minutes or until golden.

Leave the cake to cool in the tin for 5 minutes then cut into 12 bars. Transfer to a wire rack to cool completely.

**Makes 12 bars**

## Chocolate Nut Cookies

250 g (8 oz) plain flour
1 teaspoon baking powder
125 g (4 oz) butter
175 g (6 oz) caster sugar
50 g (2 oz) milk chocolate drops
25 g (1 oz) hazelnuts, toasted and coarsely chopped
1 teaspoon vanilla extract
1 egg, beaten

Sift the flour and baking powder into a bowl and rub in the butter until the mixture resembles fine breadcrumbs. Stir in the sugar, chocolate and nuts. Add the vanilla extract and egg and mix to a dough.

Knead the dough lightly on a floured surface then roll into a sausage shape, 5 cm (2 inch) in diameter. Wrap and chill until firm, about 30 minutes.

Slice into rounds about 1 cm (½ inch) thick and arrange well spaced apart on greased baking sheets. Bake in a preheated oven, 190°C (375°F), Gas Mark 5, for 10–12 minutes or until pale golden (the cookies will set as they cool).

Leave the cookies to set for about 2 minutes on the baking sheets then transfer to a wire rack to cool.

**Makes about 40**

## Fudge Brownies

125 g (4 oz) butter
90 g (3½ oz) plain chocolate, chopped
125 g (4 oz) caster sugar
125 g (4 oz) self-raising flour
50 g (2 oz) raisins
2 eggs
2 tablespoons milk

Grease and line a 20 cm (8 inch) square tin. Melt the butter and chocolate in a saucepan, stirring occasionally. Sift the sugar and flour into a bowl and add the raisins. Make a well in the centre and pour in the eggs and milk. When well mixed, fold in the chocolate mixture. Spoon the mixture into the prepared tin and bake in a preheated oven, 180°C (350°F), Gas Mark 4, for 35–40 minutes. Leave to cool for 5 minutes then transfer to a wire rack to cool completely. Cut into about 16 squares to serve.

**Makes about 16**

*right: chocolate nut cookies
chocolate and oat bars*

# Chocolate Shortbread

125 g (4 oz) butter, softened
50 g (2 oz) caster sugar
140 g (4½ oz) plain flour
20 g (¾ oz) cocoa powder
20 g (¾ oz) semolina
50 g (2 oz) white chocolate, melted,
  to decorate, (optional)

Cream the butter with the sugar in a bowl until pale and fluffy. Sift the flour, cocoa powder and semolina over the creamed mixture and work into the mixture until smooth. Press the mixture into an 18 cm (7 inch) round on a greased baking sheet. Pinch the edges for a fluted effect and lightly score into 8 wedges. Bake in a preheated oven 160°C (325°F), Gas Mark 3, for 30–35 minutes.

Leave the shortbread to cool on the baking sheet for 5 minutes then cut into wedges and transfer to a wire rack to cool completely. Drizzle with white chocolate to decorate, if liked.

**Makes 8 wedges**

*left:* chocolate shortbread
*right:* breakfast bars

# Peanut Cookies

50 g (2 oz) smooth peanut butter
50 g (2 oz) butter, softened
2 teaspoons grated orange rind
50 g (2 oz) caster sugar
40 g (1½ oz) soft light brown sugar
1 egg yolk
40 g (1½ oz) raisins
125 g (4 oz) self-raising flour
25 g (1 oz) unsalted peanuts,
   chopped

Beat together the peanut butter and butter until combined. Add the orange rind and sugars to the bowl and cream together. Add the egg yolk, raisins and flour and stir together. Roll walnut sized pieces of dough into balls and arrange, well spaced apart, on greased baking sheets. Using the back of a fork, flatten the balls lightly and sprinkle with the chopped peanuts. Bake in a preheated oven, 180°C (350°F), Gas Mark 4, for about 25 minutes, or until golden.

Leave to cool on the baking sheet for 2 minutes then transfer to a wire rack to cool completely.

## Makes about 20

# Breakfast Bars

2 tablespoons clear honey
125 g (4 oz) butter
25 g (1 oz) soft light brown sugar
125 g (4 oz) rolled oats
25 g (1 oz) raisins
25 g (1 oz) sultanas
25 g (1 oz) ready-to-eat dried
   apricots, chopped
25 g (1 oz) sunflower seeds
25 g (1 oz) sesame seeds

Put the honey, butter and sugar into a pan and heat gently until the sugar has dissolved. Stir in all the remaining ingredients and press into a shallow 18 cm (7 inch) square tin. Bake in a preheated oven, 180°C (350°F), Gas Mark 4, for 20–25 minutes or until pale golden brown. Cool for 5 minutes in the tin then mark into 12 bars. Transfer to a wire rack to cool completely.

## Makes 12

# Orange and Sultana Fruit Loaf

200 ml (7 fl oz) milk
1 teaspoon bicarbonate of soda
50 g (2 oz) butter
200 g (7 oz) plain flour
25 g (1 oz) bran
½ teaspoon cinnamon

125 g (4 oz) soft light brown sugar
250 g (8 oz) sultanas
50 g (2 oz) walnuts, chopped
rind and juice of ½ orange

**Topping:**
2 tablespoons marmalade, melted
walnut halves

Grease and line a 500 g (1 lb) loaf tin. Whisk together the milk and bicarbonate of soda to dissolve the soda. Stir in all the remaining ingredients, mixing well. Spoon the mixture into the prepared tin and bake in a preheated oven, 160°C (325°F), Gas Mark 3, for 2 hours or until risen and a skewer inserted into the loaf comes out clean. Leave to cool then brush with marmalade and decorate with walnuts.

**Makes a 500 g (1 lb) loaf**

# Applenut Spice Squares

125 g (4 oz) plain flour
1 teaspoon bicarbonate of soda
½ teaspoon mixed spice
50 g (2 oz) butter
125 g (4 oz) golden caster sugar
1 egg, beaten
50 g (2 oz) walnuts, coarsely chopped
75 g (3 oz) sultanas
150 ml (¼ pint) apple sauce
**Icing:**
50 g (2 oz) icing sugar

Grease and base-line an 18 cm (7 inch) square tin. Sift the flour, bicarbonate of soda and mixed spice into a mixing bowl. Work the butter into the flour mixture with the sugar. Add the egg, walnuts, sultanas and apple sauce. Spoon the mixture into the prepared tin. Bake in a preheated oven, 180°C (350°F), Gas Mark 4, for about 45 minutes or until golden and springy to the touch.

Leave the cake to cool in the tin then transfer to a wire rack. To make the icing, sift the icing sugar with a little water. Drizzle over the cake then cut it into squares.

## Makes about 14

# Nutty Orange Flapjacks

125 g (4 oz) butter
50 g (2 oz) demerara sugar
2 tablespoons clear honey
175 g (6 oz) rolled oats
25 g (1 oz) blanched almonds, chopped
finely grated rind of 1 orange

Grease an 18 cm (7 inch) square tin. Heat the butter, sugar and honey in a saucepan until the sugar has dissolved. Remove the pan from the heat and stir in the oats, almonds and orange rind. Spoon the mixture into the prepared tin and bake in a preheated oven, 190°C (375°F), Gas Mark 5, for 25 minutes.

Leave to cool in the tin for 5 minutes then cut into squares. Cool on a wire rack.

## Makes about 14

*left: orange and sultana fruit loaf*
*above: applenut spice squares; nutty orange flapjacks*

# Iced Cup Cakes

125 g (4 oz) butter, softened
125 g (4 oz) caster sugar
2 eggs
150 g (5 oz) self-raising flour
1 teaspoon baking powder
**To decorate:**
250 g (8 oz) icing sugar
1 tablespoon fresh lemon juice
about 2 tablespoons warm water
small sweets such as jelly tots or
    chocolate beans

Cream the butter and sugar in a bowl until light and fluffy. Gradually beat in the eggs. Sift the flour and baking powder and fold into the creamed mixture. Divide the mixture between 20 paper cases set in patty tins. Bake in a preheated oven, 190°C (375°F), Gas Mark 5, for 15–20 minutes or until risen and springy to the touch. Leave the cakes to cool on a wire rack.

Sift the icing sugar and work in the lemon juice and sufficient warm water to make a fairly stiff icing. Carefully spoon the icing over the cakes and decorate each one with a small sweet.

**Makes 20**

# Carrot Squares

175 g (6 oz) self-raising flour
50 g (2 oz) self-raising wholemeal
    flour
2 teaspoons baking powder
150 g (5 oz) soft light brown sugar
175 g (6 oz) carrot, grated
1 ripe banana, mashed
2 eggs, beaten
150 ml (¼ pint) sunflower oil
**Filling:**
50 g (2 oz) butter, softened
50 g (2 oz) cream cheese
50 g (2 oz) icing sugar
few drops vanilla extract

Grease and base-line an 18 cm (7 inch) square cake tin. Sift the flours in a bowl with the baking powder. Gradually beat in all the remaining ingredients until smooth. Spoon into the prepared tin. Bake in a preheated oven, 180°C (350°F), Gas Mark 4, for about 45 minutes or until well risen and cooked through. Turn the cake on to a wire rack to cool.

To make the filling, beat the butter until smooth then add the cream cheese and beat again. Sift the icing sugar and gradually work it into the cheese mixture. Stir in the vanilla. Cut the cake in half horizontally and spread the filling on the base, put the top back on and serve cut into squares.

**Makes 12**

# Coconut Fingers

125 g (4 oz) butter, softened
125 g (4 oz) caster sugar
2 eggs, beaten
125 g (4 oz) self-raising flour
1 teaspoon lemon juice
**Topping:**
2 egg whites
75 g (3 oz) demerara sugar
75 g (3 oz) desiccated coconut

Grease and line a 30 x 20 cm (12 x 8 inch) Swiss roll tin. Cream the butter and sugar in a bowl until pale and fluffy. Gradually beat in the eggs. Fold in the flour and lemon juice. Spoon the mixture into the prepared tin.

Whisk the egg whites until stiff and gradually whisk in the sugar and fold in the coconut. Spoon evenly over the cake mixture. Bake in a preheated oven, 180°C (350°F), Gas Mark 4, for about 30 minutes or until the mixture is risen and spongy. Turn on to a wire rack to cool. Serve cut into fingers.

**Makes 20**

*right:* jammy buns

# Jammy Buns

250 g (8 oz) self-raising
  flour
pinch of cinnamon
50 g (2 oz) butter, diced
50 g (2 oz) caster sugar
1 egg, beaten
2 tablespoons milk
2 tablespoons strawberry jam
1 tablespoon granulated sugar

Sift the flour and cinnamon into a bowl, add the butter and rub in until the mixture resembles breadcrumbs. Add the sugar, egg and sufficient milk to give a firm dough. Knead the dough lightly on a floured surface until smooth.

Divide the mixture into 12 even sized pieces and roll into balls. Using a lightly floured finger make a well in each ball and spoon in a little jam. Pinch the edges together to enclose the jam. Set the buns, join-side down, on lightly greased baking sheets and sprinkle with sugar. Bake in a preheated oven, 190°C (375°F), Gas Mark 5, for about 10 minutes, until pale golden.

Leave the buns to set on the baking sheet for 1 minute. Transfer to a wire rack to cool completely.

**Makes 12**

# Lemon Surprise Cake

175 g (6 oz) butter, softened
175 g (6 oz) caster sugar
grated rind and juice of 2 lemons
3 eggs, beaten
175 g (6 oz) self-raising flour
**Filling:**
25 g (1 oz) butter
25 g (1 oz) demerara sugar
75 g (3 oz) sultanas
25 g (1 oz) glacé cherries,
    chopped
grated rind of 1 lemon

**To decorate:**
icing sugar, for sifting
sugared lemon halves

Grease and base-line an 18 cm
(7 inch) round cake tin.

Prepare the filling. Heat the butter
and sugar in a saucepan until the
sugar has dissolved. Remove from
the heat and stir in the sultanas,
cherries and lemon rind. Set aside.

Cream the butter and sugar in a
bowl until pale and fluffy. Gradually
beat in the lemon rind and juice
with the eggs, adding a little flour if
the mixture begins to curdle. Fold
in the remaining flour. Spoon half

the mixture into the prepared tin,
sprinkle with half the fruit filling
mixture. Repeat with the remaining
cake and filling mixtures. Bake in a
preheated oven, 180°C (350°F), Gas
Mark 4, for about 1 hour, or until
well risen and golden – cover with
foil towards the end of cooking to
prevent burning. Leave to stand for
5 minutes then turn on to a wire
rack and leave to cool completely.

Dust the cake with icing sugar and
decorate with the lemon halves.

## Makes an 18 cm (7 inch) cake

# Gingerbread Ring

125 g (4 oz) butter

125 g (4 oz) soft light brown sugar

175 g (6 oz) black treacle

250 g (8 oz) plain flour

1 tablespoon ground ginger

½ teaspoon cinnamon

1 egg, beaten

½ teaspoon bicarbonate of soda

6 tablespoons milk

**Icing:**

125 g (4 oz) icing sugar, sifted

2 teaspoons ginger syrup

1 tablespoon warm water

Grease and flour a 20 cm (8 inch) ring mould.

Heat the butter, sugar and treacle in a saucepan until the sugar has dissolved. Sift together the flour, ginger and cinnamon and stir in the melted mixture with the egg. Dissolve the bicarbonate of soda in the milk and stir into the batter. Carefully pour into the prepared tin and bake in a preheated oven, 180°C (350°F), Gas Mark 4, for about 1 hour or until the mixture is risen and just beginning to shrink from the sides of the tin.

Leave the cake in the tin for 2 minutes then turn on to a wire rack to cool completely.

To make the icing, mix together all the ingredients and drizzle over the ginger ring.

**Makes a 20 cm (8 inch) ring cake**

# Banana Chocolate Slices

50 g (2 oz) butter, softened

50 g (2 oz) soft light brown sugar

2 large ripe bananas, mashed

2 tablespoons cocoa powder

1 tablespoon drinking chocolate

150 g (5 oz) carton natural yogurt

1 egg, beaten

175 g (6 oz) wholemeal flour

2 teaspoons baking powder

25 g (1 oz) crunchy oat cereal

1 tablespoon demerara sugar

Grease and base-line an 18 cm (7 inch) square cake tin. Cream the butter and sugar in a bowl until pale and fluffy. Beat in the bananas, cocoa, drinking chocolate, yogurt and egg. Mix well, then fold in the flour and baking powder. Spoon into the prepared tin and sprinkle the cereal and sugar over the surface. Bake in a preheated oven, 180°C (350°F), Gas Mark 4, for about 40 minutes or until the mixture is risen and just firm. Leave in the tin for about 10 minutes then turn on to a wire rack to cool completely. Serve cut into slices.

**Makes an 18 cm (7 inch) square cake**

# Crispy Crackles

50 g (2 oz) butter

2 tablespoons golden syrup

50 g (2 oz) drinking chocolate

50 g (2 oz) cornflakes

Heat the butter and syrup in a saucepan until melted. Stir in the drinking chocolate and cornflakes. Spoon the mixture into paper cake cases set in patty tins. Leave to set.

**Makes 16**

*left: lemon surprise cake*
**above:** *crispy crackles*

# Chocolate Carrot and Raisin Cake

150 g (5 oz) soft light brown sugar
125 g (4 oz) butter
175 g (6 oz) carrots, grated
125 g (4 oz) raisins
250 ml (8 fl oz) water
250 g (8 oz) wholemeal flour
25 g (1 oz) cocoa powder
½ teaspoon grated nutmeg
50 g (2 oz) ground almonds
2 teaspoons baking powder
1 egg, beaten

**Topping:**
125 g (4 oz) cream cheese
125 g (4 oz) fromage frais
2 teaspoons clear honey
shredded orange rind

Grease and base-line a 20 cm (8 inch) cake tin. Put the sugar, butter, carrots, raisins and water into a saucepan. Bring to the boil and boil for 5 minutes. Leave to cool.

Mix the flour, cocoa, nutmeg, almonds and baking powder in a bowl, make a well in the centre and add the carrot mixture with the egg and beat well. Spoon the mixture into the prepared tin. Bake in a preheated oven, 190°C (375°F), Gas Mark 5, for about 40 minutes, or until risen and firm. Turn the cake on to a wire rack to cool.

To make the topping, beat the cream cheese then add the fromage frais and honey. Swirl the icing on top of the cake and scatter with the shredded orange rind.

**Makes a 20 cm (8 inch) cake**

# Chocolate Fudge Cake

25 g (1 oz) cocoa powder

1 tablespoon instant coffee granules

125 ml (4 fl oz) hot water

125 g (4 oz) butter, softened

125 g (4 oz) soft light brown sugar

3 eggs, beaten

75 g (3 oz) plain chocolate, melted

250 g (8 oz) self-raising wholemeal flour

**Icing:**

250 g (8 oz) crème fraîche

75 g (3 oz) plain chocolate, melted

**To decorate:**

75 g (3 oz) plain chocolate, melted

Grease and base-line a 20 cm (8 inch) cake tin. Stir together the cocoa and coffee and mix to a paste with the hot water. Cream the butter and sugar in a bowl until light and fluffy. Gradually beat in the eggs. Fold in the cocoa mixture, melted chocolate and flour. Spoon into the prepared tin and bake in a preheated oven, 180°C (350°F), Gas Mark 4, for about 35 minutes, or until the cake is well risen and firm. Turn on to a wire rack to cool.

Beat the crème fraîche and melted chocolate until smooth. Cut the cooled cake in half horizontally and use half the icing to sandwich it together. Use the remaining icing to coat the top and sides of the cake.

Thinly spread the melted chocolate on to a cool dry work surface and leave to set for about 30 minutes. Draw a knife or cheese slice across the chocolate to make scrolls. Scatter the scrolls on top of the cake. Serve in thin slices.

**Makes a 20 cm (8 inch) cake**

# Mocha Swiss Roll

1 tablespoon instant coffee granules

1 tablespoon hot water

3 eggs

75 g (3 oz) caster sugar, plus extra for sifting

65 g (2 ½ oz) plain flour

15 g (½ oz) cocoa powder

**Filling:**

50 g (2 oz) butter, softened

50 g (2 oz) plain chocolate, melted

50 g (2 oz) icing sugar, sifted

Grease and line a 30 x 20 cm (12 x 8 inch) Swiss roll tin.

Stir the coffee and water until the coffee dissolves. Whisk the eggs and caster sugar until thick enough to leave a ribbon-like trail when the whisks are lifted. Sift the flour and cocoa over the mixture and fold in carefully with the coffee liquid. Spoon into the prepared tin. Bake in a preheated oven, 200°C (400°F), Gas Mark 6, for 10–12 minutes or until springy to the touch.

Meanwhile, sprinkle a sheet of greaseproof paper with caster sugar. When the cake is cooked, carefully turn it on to the greaseproof paper. Peel off the lining paper, trim the edges of the cake and carefully roll up the cake and paper. Leave to cool.

To make the filling, beat the butter until smooth then stir in the chocolate and icing sugar. Carefully unroll the cooled cake and spread with the chocolate icing, then reroll the cake, discarding the paper.

**Serves 8**

*left: mocha swiss roll*
*right: banana and apple slices*

# Banana and Apple Slices

125 g (4 oz) butter

150 g (5 oz) soft light brown
sugar

2 eggs

275 g (9 oz) self-raising wholemeal
flour

2 dessert apples, cored, peeled and
grated

2 bananas, mashed

75 g (3 oz) sultanas

125 ml (4 fl oz) apple juice

Grease and base-line a 20 cm
(8 inch) square tin.

Cream the butter and sugar in a
bowl until light and fluffy.
Gradually beat in the eggs. Fold in
the flour, apples, bananas, sultanas
and apple juice. Spoon the mixture
into the prepared tin. Bake in a
preheated oven, 180°C (350°F), Gas
Mark 4, for about 40 minutes or
until risen and springy to the touch.

Turn the cake on to a wire rack
and leave to cool. Serve cut into
fingers or squares.

**Makes 16**

# Anzac Cookies

2 tablespoons golden syrup

125 g (4 oz) butter

125 g (4 oz) caster sugar

125 g (4 oz) plain flour

75 g (3 oz) rolled oats

50 g (2 oz) desiccated coconut

2 teaspoons bicarbonate of soda

1 tablespoon hot water

Put the syrup, butter and sugar into
a saucepan and heat gently until
the sugar has dissolved.

Remove the pan from the heat
and sift in the flour then add the
oats and coconut and beat together.
Dissolve the bicarbonate of soda in
the water and add to the coconut
mixture. Leave to stand until cool
enough to handle.

Roll walnut sized pieces of dough
into balls and arrange spaced apart
on greased baking sheets. Bake in a
preheated oven, 180°C (350°F), Gas
Mark 4, for 20 minutes or until the
cookies are golden brown.

Leave the cookies on the baking
sheets for about 2 minutes then
transfer to a wire rack to cool
completely.

**Makes about 30**

# Chequered Chocolate Cake

125 g (4 oz) plain flour
125 g (4 oz) wholemeal flour
25 g (1 oz) cocoa powder
150 g (5 oz) caster sugar
2 teaspoons baking powder
½ teaspoon bicarbonate of soda
125 g (4 oz) butter, melted
200 ml (7 fl oz) milk
3 eggs
1½ tablespoons black treacle
**Icing:**
175 g (6 oz) butter, softened
300 g (10 oz) icing sugar, sifted
75 g (3 oz) plain chocolate, melted
1 teaspoon vanilla extract
**To decorate:**
75 g (3 oz) plain chocolate, melted
75 g (3 oz) white chocolate, melted

Grease and base-line a 23 cm (9 inch) square cake tin. Sift the flours into a bowl with the cocoa, sugar, baking powder and bicarbonate of soda. Make a well in the centre and beat in the butter, milk, eggs and treacle.

Spoon the mixture into the prepared tin and bake in a preheated oven, 160°C (325°F), Gas Mark 3, for about 40 minutes until risen and just shrinking from the sides of the tin. Turn the cake on to a wire rack to cool.

Meanwhile, make the icing, Beat the butter until light and fluffy, then gradually add the sifted icing sugar. Put half the mixture into another bowl. Add the melted chocolate to one bowl and beat until smooth. Beat the vanilla extract into the second bowl.

Cut the cake in half horizontally and spread the cut side of one half with a little chocolate icing. Spread a little vanilla icing on the cut side of the second half. Sandwich the cake together and spread the sides with chocolate icing and the top with vanilla icing.

Spread the plain chocolate thinly on a sheet of baking parchment or waxed paper and leave to set. Repeat with the white chocolate. Using a warm knife cut both the chocolates into squares and arrange on top of the cake alternating plain and white squares.

## Makes a 23 cm (9 inch) square cake

# Hot Apple Muffins

250 g (8 oz) plain flour
1 tablespoon baking powder
50 g (2 oz) golden caster sugar
½ teaspoon cinnamon
½ teaspoon ground ginger
2 eggs, beaten
150 ml (¼ pint) buttermilk
50 g (2 oz) butter, melted
250 g (8 oz) cooking apples, peeled, cored and finely chopped

Sift the flour, baking powder, sugar, cinnamon and ground ginger into a bowl. Beat the eggs with the buttermilk and butter and beat into the sifted mixture. Fold in the chopped apple. Divide the mixture between 24 paper muffin cases set in muffin tins. Bake in a preheated oven, 220°C (425°F), Gas Mark 7, for 15–20 minutes or until well risen and golden brown. Serve the muffins warm.

## Makes 24

# Crunchy Date Layer

125 g (4 oz) wholemeal flour
150 g (5 oz) rolled oats
250 g (8 oz) butter
**Filling:**
250 g (8 oz) dates, pitted and
  chopped
2 tablespoons water
1 teaspoon bicarbonate of soda
1 tablespoon orange juice
1 tablespoon clear honey

Grease an 18 cm (7 inch) square tin.

First prepare the filling. Put the dates into a pan with the water and bicarbonate of soda. Simmer for about 5 minutes until the dates have softened. Remove from the heat and add the orange juice and honey.

Stir together the flour and oats in a bowl, then rub in the butter. Press half the oat mixture into the base of the prepared tin. Spread the date mixture on top and gently press the remaining oat mixture over that. Bake in a preheated oven, 180°C (350°F), Gas Mark 4, for about 20 minutes, or until pale golden. Leave the cake to stand for 10 minutes then mark into about 14 squares. Turn on to a wire rack to cool completely.

**Makes about 14 squares**

# American Banana Loaf

250 g (8 oz) self-raising flour
125 g (4 oz) butter
175 g (6 oz) golden caster sugar
1 teaspoon lemon juice
3 tablespoons milk
2 bananas, mashed
1 teaspoon finely grated lemon rind
2 eggs, beaten

Grease and base-line a 1 kg (2 lb) loaf tin.

Sift the flour into a mixing bowl then rub in the butter until the mixture resembles fine breadcrumbs. Mix in the sugar. Stir together the lemon juice, milk, bananas, lemon rind and eggs. Work the banana mixture into the rubbed in mixture, until smooth.

Spoon the mixture into the tin and bake in a preheated oven, 180°C (350°F), Gas Mark 4, for 1 hour or until the loaf is well risen and just shrinking from the sides of the tin. Turn the loaf on to a wire rack to cool.

**Makes 1 loaf**

# Whisked Sponge Cake

250 g (8 oz) caster sugar
3 eggs
50 g (2 oz) butter, melted
3 tablespoons warm water
½ teaspoon vanilla extract
150 g (5 oz) plain flour
5 tablespoons strawberry jam
icing sugar, for dusting

Grease and base-line two 18 cm (7 inch) sandwich tins.

Whisk the sugar and eggs in a bowl until a ribbon-like trail forms when the whisks are lifted. Fold in the butter, water and vanilla. Sift the flour over the mixture and fold in gently. Divide the mixture between the prepared tins and bake in a preheated oven, 190°C (375°F), Gas Mark 5, for about 20 minutes or until well risen and springy to the touch.

Turn the sponges on to a wire rack to cool. Sandwich the sponges together with the jam and dust with sifted icing sugar.

**Makes an 18 cm (7 inch) round cake**

# Caramel Shortbread

**Base:**

250 g (8 oz) butter

125 g (4 oz) caster sugar

300 g (10 oz) plain flour

**Filling:**

250 g (8 oz) butter

125 g (4 oz) caster sugar

400 g (13 oz) can condensed milk

4 tablespoons golden syrup

**Topping:**

250 g (8 oz) plain chocolate, chopped

25 g (1 oz) butter

Cream the butter with the sugar until fluffy, then work in the flour. Knead lightly in a bowl then press into the base of a 30 x 20 x 2.5 cm (12 x 8 x 1 inch) tin. Bake in a preheated oven, 180°C (350°F), Gas Mark 4, for 25 minutes or until golden and crisp. Leave to cool in the tin.

Meanwhile, prepare the filling. Put all the ingredients into a saucepan and cook gently, stirring constantly, until melted and smooth. Bring to the boil and cook for 3–5 minutes, still stirring, until golden. Quickly pour over the shortbread and leave to cool.

To make the topping, melt the chocolate and butter in a bowl set over a pan of simmering water. Pour the chocolate mixture over the cooled and set caramel. Leave to set in a cool place then cut into squares, triangles or bars.

## Makes about 30 pieces

*above: caramel shortbread*

# Party Food

## Animal Open Sandwiches

6 thin slices of brown bread
75 g (3 oz) cream cheese
yeast extract, for spreading
125 g (4 oz) plain potato crisps
mustard and cress, to serve

Spread the bread with the cream cheese then the yeast extract. Crush the crisps whilst in the packet and sprinkle over the yeast extract. Use animal-shaped cutters to make the open sandwiches. Serve on a plate scattered with mustard and cress.

**Makes about 24 sandwiches**

## Martian Base Salmon Dip

250 g (8 oz) poached salmon, free of skin and bone
150 g (5 oz) carton natural yogurt
1 tablespoon tomato purée
1 tablespoon fresh lemon juice
7.5 cm (3 inch) piece of cucumber, diced
1 tablespoon chopped dill
salt and pepper
**To serve:**
vegetable crudités
breadsticks

Using a fork, flake the salmon, then stir in the yogurt and tomato purée. Season with salt, pepper and lemon juice. Stir in the cucumber and dill just before serving. Serve the dip with crudités and breadsticks for dipping.

**Serves 8**

## Cheesy Sausage Rolls

375 g (12 oz) shortcrust pastry
125 g (4 oz) red Leicester cheese, finely grated
300 g (10 oz) good quality sausagemeat
2 tablespoons chopped parsley
salt and pepper
egg yolk, to glaze

Roll out the pastry thin. Trim to a large rectangle and cut in half lengthways. Sprinkle the centre strip of each rectangle with the cheese. Beat the sausagemeat and parsley and season with salt and pepper. Divide the sausagemeat mixture in half and roll each piece to fit the length of the pastry. Sit the sausages on the cheese. Brush the edges of the pastry with a little egg yolk and fold to enclose the sausagemeat. Press to seal the pastry. Cut each strip into 12 and score the top lightly. Brush with egg yolk.

Arrange the sausage rolls on baking sheets and bake in a preheated oven, 190°C (375°F), Gas Mark 5, for about 20 minutes or until they are golden and cooked through. Serve warm.

**Makes 24**

# Saucy Sausages

8 cocktail sausages
4 teaspoons sweet pickle
8 rashers of rindless streaky bacon

Cut the sausages lengthways until almost in half. Spoon a little pickle down the centre of each one. Wrap the bacon around the sausages. Cook the sausages under a preheated grill for about 15 minutes, turning frequently, until the bacon and sausages are cooked through. Serve warm.

**Makes 8**

# Moon Dip

2 large ripe bananas
1 tablespoon fresh lemon juice
250 g (8 oz) carton Greek-style
   yogurt with honey
**To serve:**
apple wedges, dipped in lemon juice
banana wedges, dipped in lemon
   juice
orange segments

Peel the bananas and mash with the lemon juice. Stir in the yogurt.

**Serves 8**

# Shuttle Dip

4 eggs, hard boiled
125 g (4 oz) cream cheese
2 tablespoons natural yogurt
2 teaspoons tomato ketchup
salt and freshly ground black pepper
**To serve:**
vegetable crudités
bread sticks

Mash the peeled eggs and stir in the remaining ingredients.

**Serves 8**

*below: saucy sausages*

# Cheese Twist Rings

125 g (4 oz) puff pastry
50 g (2 oz) red Leicester cheese,
  finely grated
1 egg, beaten
2 tablespoons sesame seeds

Roll out the pastry thinly to a 30 cm (12 inch) square. Sprinkle the cheese on to one half of the pastry then fold over the pastry and roll gently to seal. Brush with beaten egg and sprinkle with sesame seeds.

Cut 24 thin strips of pastry and twist loosely and form into rings. Arrange on baking sheets and bake in a preheated oven, 220°C (425°F), Gas Mark 7, for about 12 minutes or until golden and puffy. Cool on wire racks.

**Makes 24**

# Sausage Caterpillar

12 cocktail sausages
2 tablespoons maple syrup
6 rashers of rindless streaky bacon,
  halved crossways
4 pineapple rings, each cut into
  3 pieces
125 g (4 oz) Cheddar cheese, cut into
  12 squares
1 mandarin, separated into segments
1 large cucumber
2 cherries

Arrange the sausages on a grill pan and drizzle with maple syrup. Place the under a preheated, moderate grill for about 15 minutes, turning occasionally, until golden and cooked through. Wrap the bacon around the pieces of pineapple and grill for about 4 minutes on each side or until the bacon is cooked. Put cocktail sticks through each sausage, bacon wrapped pineapple and cube of cheese and mandarin segment.

Trim the cucumber so it stands flat and cut a mouth shape on the front. Fix the cherries to the cucumber with cocktail sticks, to resemble eyes. Stick the bacon wrapped pineapple on the sides of the cucumber, the cheese and mandarin segments above and the sausages in a line down the middle.

**Serves 12**

# Pepperoni Pizza Faces

140 g (4½ oz) packet pizza base mix
6 tablespoons warm water
**Topping:**
6 tablespoons tomato pizza topping
50 g (2 oz) button mushrooms, sliced
½ pepperoni stick
18 peas
75 g (3 oz) Cheddar cheese, grated
1 tablespoon olive oil

Prepare the pizza base according to packet instructions. Knead the dough and divide it into 8 pieces, then pat or roll them into rounds. Spread with the pizza topping. Add slices of mushroom for noses, slices of pepperoni for mouths, peas for eyes and scatter cheese around the top to resemble hair. Leave in a warm place for about 15 minutes.

Drizzle the pizza faces with oil and bake in a preheated oven, 200°C (400°F), Gas Mark 6, for about 15 minutes, or until the bases are crispy and the cheese is bubbling.

**Makes 8**

*right:* sausage caterpillar,
*pepperoni pizza faces*

# Butterfly Wings

3 egg yolks
50 g (2 oz) caster sugar
120 ml (4 fl oz) single cream
2 teaspoons vanilla extract
250 g (8 oz) plain flour
sunflower oil, for frying
icing sugar, for sprinkling

Beat together the egg yolks, sugar, cream and vanilla extract. Work in the flour to give a stiff dough. Knead lightly on a floured surface. Roll out the dough thinly and cut into 24 diamond shapes, about 7 cm (3 inches) across. Make a small slit across each diamond and carefully tuck the points of the diamond through the cut and pull slightly.

Heat the oil in a saucepan and cook the dough, in batches, for about 3–4 minutes or until golden. Drain well on kitchen paper and sprinkle the butterfly wings with sifted icing sugar to serve.

## Makes 24

# Fruit Kebabs

150 ml (¼ pint) fresh orange juice
juice of 2 lemons
50 g (2 oz) caster sugar
1 pear, peeled, cored and cut
    into 8 pieces
2 small firm bananas, each cut
    into 4 pieces
2 slices of pineapple, peeled and cut
    into chunks
8 seedless white grapes
2 tablespoons clear honey
**Coconut cream:**
300 ml (½ pint) double cream
3 tablespoons coconut milk

Stir together the orange and lemon juice, then sprinkle in the sugar. Add the fruit and stir to coat evenly. Thread the sugar-coated fruits on to 8 kebab skewers. Arrange the skewers on a grill pan and brush with the honey. Cook the fruits under a preheated, moderate grill for about 4 minutes, turning the skewers and brushing them with more honey, until the fruits are lightly caramelized.

Meanwhile, beat the cream and coconut milk until lightly whipped. Serve the kebabs warm with the coconut cream.

## Makes 8

# Party Letters

200 g (7 oz) self-raising flour
1 tablespoon caster sugar
1 egg, beaten
300 ml (½ pint) milk
maple syrup, to serve

Sift the flour and sugar into a bowl and make a well in the centre. Stir the egg and milk together and pour into the well in the flour, then gradually whisk to make a smooth batter.

Heat a large non-.stick pan or griddle. Spoon the batter into letter shapes – making sure you have all the initials of the party guests. Cook the letters in batches. When bubbles begin to appear on the surface of the batter, carefully turn them over and cook until golden on the second side. Serve warm with maple syrup for drizzling over.

## Makes about 12

# Coconut Funny Faces

75g (3 oz) butter, softened

75 g (3 oz) caster sugar

3 egg yolks

½ teaspoon vanilla extract

125 g (4 oz) plain flour

50 g (2 oz ) rice flour

75 g (3 oz) desiccated coconut

**To decorate:**

6 tablespoons lemon curd

4 tablespoons desiccated or long
  shred coconut

1 tablespoon cocoa powder

3 glacé cherries

30 small jelly sweets

Cream the butter and sugar in a bowl until light and fluffy. Beat in the egg yolks and vanilla. Sift in the flours and stir into the creamed mixture with the coconut. Knead lightly then chill for 10 minutes.

Roll out the dough on a lightly floured surface and stamp out about 24 rounds using a 7.5 cm (3 inch) cutter. Arrange the rounds on greased baking sheets and bake in a preheated oven, 180°C (350°F), Gas Mark 4, for 12–15 minutes, or until pale golden.

Leave on the baking sheets for 1 minute then transfer to a wire rack to cool.

Sandwich together the biscuit rounds with some of the lemon curd. Spread a little lemon curd around the edge of the top biscuit. Mix together the coconut and cocoa and sprinkle over the lemon curd. Use slithers of cherry to represent a mouth and arrange sweets as eyes and half a sweet as a nose.

## Makes 12

*above: party letters*

# Stripy Jelly

135 g (4½ oz) packet lemon jelly, torn
  into cubes

135 g (4½ oz) packet raspberry jelly,
  torn into cubes

1½ x 135 g (4½ oz) packets lime jelly,
  torn into cubes

2 bananas

2 apples

4 oranges

250 g (8 oz) seedless grapes

Dissolve the lemon and raspberry jellies, separately, in 300 ml (½ pint) boiling water, then make each up to 475 ml (16 fl oz) with cold water. Pour the lemon jelly into 12 wetted fluted jelly moulds. Chill until almost set. Leave the raspberry jelly to stand then spoon on top of the lemon jelly. Make up the lime jelly but make the liquid up to 750 ml (1¼ pints). When this lime liquid is cool pour it over the raspberry jelly.

Peel and slice the bananas, core and chop the apple. Peel and segment the orange, chop coarsely, halve the grapes. Mix the fruits together and carefully spoon them into the moulds before the lime jelly sets. Chill until set. Quickly dip the base of the moulds in hot water then turn them out onto plates.

**Serves 12**

# Orange Cup Trifles

8 oranges, with unblemished skins
4 trifle sponges
400 g (13 oz) can pear halves
135 g (4½ oz) packet lemon jelly, torn
    into cubes
300 ml (½ pint) double cream
orange and lemon shreds, to decorate

Slice the tops from the oranges and scoop out and chop the orange flesh (keep the orange skins whole). Cut the trifle sponges into cubes. Drain and chop the pear halves, reserving the juice. Stir together the chopped orange, sponge and pears and spoon them into the orange shells. Put the jelly into a measuring jug and pour over 300 ml (½ pint) boiling water. Stir to dissolve the jelly then add the reserved pear juice to make up the liquid to 575 ml (18 fl oz). Leave the jelly until almost set then spoon it into the orange cups. Leave to set.

Lightly whip the cream and spoon it on top of the trifles. Decorate with orange and lemon shreds.

**Serves 8**

*left: stripy jelly*

# Gingerbread Ducks

170 g (6 oz) plain flour
½ teaspoon bicarbonate of soda
1½ teaspoons ground ginger
½ teaspoon cinnamon
75 g (3 oz) butter
125 g (4 oz) soft light brown sugar
2 tablespoons golden syrup
a few currants
small pieces of orange jelly sweets

Sift the flour, bicarbonate of soda, ginger and cinnamon into a bowl. Heat the butter, sugar and syrup in a saucepan until the sugar dissolves. Pour into the sifted mixture and beat well until smooth. Chill for 30 minutes.

Roll out the dough on a lightly floured surface and, using a duck cutter, cut out ducks. Transfer to a greased baking sheet. Add currant eyes and a little orange jelly sweet to resemble a beak. Bake in a preheated oven, 190°C (375°F), Gas Mark 5, for 10 minutes or until golden.

Leave the ducks on the baking sheet for 2 minutes then transfer to a wire rack to cool completely.

**Makes about 12**

# Flutterby Cakes

175 g (6 oz) butter, softened
175 g (6 oz) caster sugar
3 eggs, beaten
175 g (6 oz) self raising flour
grated rind 1 lemon
3 tablespoons strawberry jam
**Icing:**
125 g (4 oz) butter, softened
175 g (6 oz) icing sugar, sifted
1 tablespoon fresh lemon juice
6 lemon flavoured jelly slices
6 orange flavoured jelly slices
3 matchmaker chocolate sticks

Grease and base line two 20 cm (8 inch) sandwich tins. Cream the butter and sugar together until fluffy. Gradually beat in the eggs. Fold in the flour and lemon rind. Divide the mixture between the tins.

Bake in a preheated oven, 190°C (375°F), Gas Mark 5, for 25 minutes until risen. Turn onto a wire rack to cool.

Prepare the icing: Beat the butter until light, beat in the icing sugar and lemon juice. Spread half the butter icing on the sponge followed by the jam. Put the second sponge on top and spread with the remaining butter icing. Use the jelly slices to represent butterfly wings and chocolate sticks as their bodies.

**Serves 12**

# Index